PAINTING SECRETS

from Brian Santos
The Wall Wizard

Meredith Books®
Des Moines, Iowa

Table of *CONTENTS*

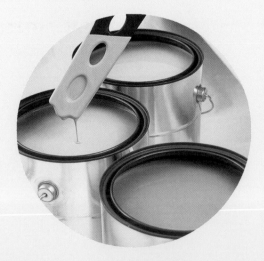

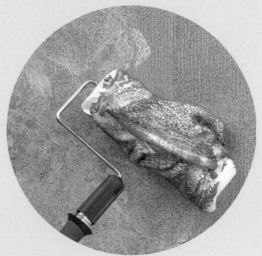

Meet *the* Wizard

Welcome to my world, the Wall Wizard's Workshop, where you are limited only by your imagination.

You've opened this book because you're interested in painting your home. You're not alone: Painting is the No. 1 project that do-it-yourselfers tackle, boosting the manufacture of paint and painting supplies into a multibillion-dollar-a-year industry. Unfortunately that industry doesn't teach you how to paint! How can you be good at something without ever being taught? It's like trying to read *War and Peace* without knowing your ABCs.

That's where the Wall Wizard can help. I've spent 25 years making mistakes; that's why I'm an expert at knowing what works and what doesn't. Throughout the following chapters, I'll teach you the fundamental principles of painting and share scores of tips, tricks, and techniques that I've learned through years of hands-on experience.

As a fourth-generation painting contractor, I learned from my father and grandfather the value of working with my hands. I helped by pasting paper, cleaning tools, and keeping the work area neat. By age 16 I was a certified apprentice, and two years later I helped found Wallpapers to Go, a successful West Coast company specializing in painting, faux finishing, and wallcoverings. After becoming a licensed finishes contractor, I discovered that people wanted to learn how to paint, faux finish, and wallpaper, but they had limited resources to teach them. That's when I began presenting painting workshops at home shows around the world. In more than 20 years of traveling, I've presented more than 5,000 workshops and reached over a million people.

My philosophy is simple: **Knowledge is power.** I use educational, entertaining, and empowering principles and processes—all captured in this book—to take the fear out of home improvement projects. My mission is to educate. The manufacturers put out great products, but they don't really tell you how to use them. Anyone can pick up a brush; the problem is knowing what to do with it.

Besides learning the basics of painting, you'll discover tips for using common household products to achieve professional results. Plastic wrap, vegetable oil spray, vanilla flavoring, plastic milk jugs, garbage bags, and fabric softener are just a few of the tools I use to produce extraordinary professional finishes—and so can you.

Even if you have never before picked up a paintbrush, you can create your own wall magic in no time. All it takes is a little planning, patience, and persistence. There is a Wizard within us all, when you learn the why behind the how-tos of painting.

When you look through Wizard eyes, you can see the magic all around you.

chapter **1**

The Magic of Color

Your home is your largest, most visible, and most expensive possession, and what color do you paint it? White! There are 16 million colors to choose from, but you wimp out and play it safe. Boring! And by the way, antique white, vanilla, and off-white are not colors.

Color is perhaps the most cost-effective and powerful tool in your decorating bag of tricks. Yet few people know the simple rules that govern this important element of design.

First understand there is absolutely no wrong color to use. Any color can be livable when the hue, value, intensity, and lighting are correct and in balance. If you want to paint a powder room purple with silver leafing and a black glaze, go for it! These color combinations used in the appropriate context, scale, and proportion can be stunning. Used inappropriately, though, they can appear garish and overwhelming.

So go ahead—experiment! If the outcome isn't what you expected, the worst thing that can happen is you'll have to paint the walls again—hardly an irreversible disaster. In this chapter, I'll explain some common myths, mistakes, and misconceptions about color. You'll learn about proven tools and techniques and be empowered with the knowledge and language of color to express your own style with skill and confidence.

COLOR COMBINATIONS
Learn the simple rules that direct your design—page **10**

CREATING A COLOR PLAN
Train your eyes to see color at work all around you—page **18**

FORMULAS FOR SUCCESS
Choose the paint that's best for your rooms—page **24**

Color BASICS

Effective design depends on the relationship of different colors in a room. Color creates a room's personality, defines its style, sets its mood, controls its space, accents its advantages, and hides its faults. It can turn a dull space into a warm, inviting environment. Yet one color alone can't achieve these benefits. You need a combination of colors that complement and reinforce a particular look or mood. This selection of color combinations becomes your decorating plan.

Changing the wall color and a few accessories creates three different looks in the same room.

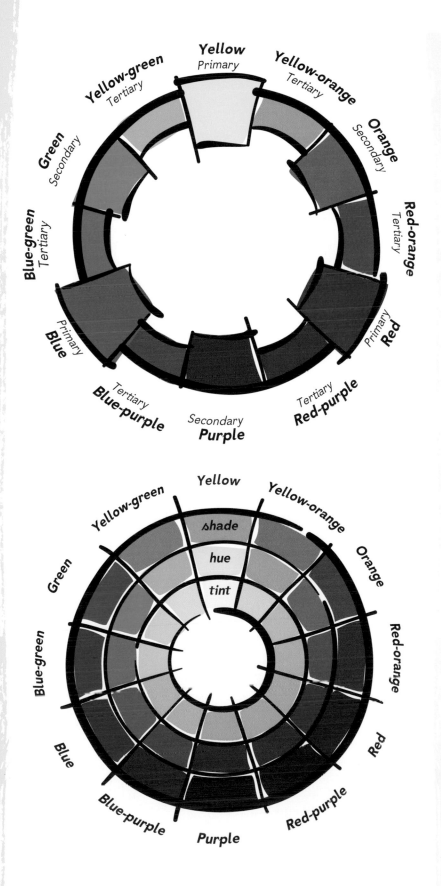

THE COLOR WHEEL

Most people haven't seen a color wheel since middle-school art class or high school home economics, but a Wall Wizard knows it is a handy design tool. A color wheel shows how colors relate to each other. Three relationships are of particular interest:

PRIMARY COLORS

The most basic of color relationships, primary colors are the three pure colors found in light: red, yellow, and blue. They cannot be broken down into other colors, but when used in various combinations, they create all other colors. Primary colors are equidistant from one another on the color wheel.

SECONDARY COLORS

The second level of colors are orange, green, and purple. Each is created from equal amounts of two primary colors. On the color wheel, each secondary color falls halfway between the two primary colors it contains and directly opposite the third primary color.

TERTIARY COLORS

Tertiary, or third-level colors, are created by combining equal parts of a primary and its adjacent secondary color. Yellow and orange, for example, form yellow-orange.

Color levels build on each other. This means you need primary colors to form secondary colors, and both to develop tertiary colors.

The bottom color wheel presents the differences among pure colors, or hues, shown in the middle ring; shades, created by adding black, shown in the outer ring; and tints, created by adding white, shown in the inner ring.

Color COMBINATIONS

The color wheel demystifies color relationships and helps you find colors that work well together. No hard-and-fast rules exist about which colors should be used together, but some natural combinations make successful matches. The following classic combinations are considered the basics for beginners.

Analogous colors. This set uses three colors located next to each other on the color wheel. Green, yellow-green, and yellow make an analogous arrangement. So do blue-green, blue, and blue-purple. Analogous colors are harmonious because the colors are closely related and your eyes pass over them easily.

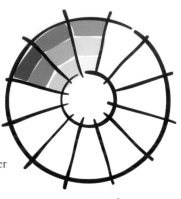

Analogous

Complementary colors. Two colors located opposite each other on the color wheel complement each other. The most common example is the red and green of Christmas. Another is blue and orange. Because a complementary plan combines exact opposites, it balances warm and cool colors. Complements stimulate one another but can seem garish if used together in full intensity.

Complementary

Triad colors. Three colors, or a triad, are spaced equally in distance from each other on the color wheel. Red, blue, and yellow are a triad, for example, as is orange, green, and purple—and there are many more. Triads form complex, lively color plans, so controlling values and intensities is important.

Triad

Split Complementary

Split complementary. This scheme combines a color plus the color on each side of its complement. Pairing yellow with blue-purple and red-purple, for example, makes a split complementary plan. The subtle shift in the complementary colors enriches the plan.

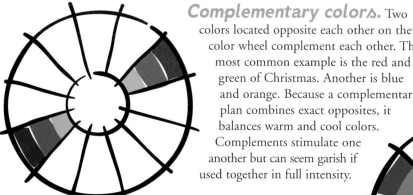

A triad of primary colors—yellow, red, and blue—creates a bold color plan that moves through adjoining rooms.

The closely related colors of this room's walls, furnishings, and accessories form an analogous plan.

Because these colors are opposite each other on the color wheel, the cool violet accents complement the warm yellows.

The following color combinations are also successful but require a little more thought, control, and balance.

Double split complementary. This plan combines four colors, one from each side of two complementary colors. It is a rich color plan but difficult to bring off successfully.

Monochromatic. In a monochromatic plan, one color is used in many values, intensities, and textures, so the mix stays lively and interesting. This sophisticated, aesthetic plan needs texture contrasts to work well.

Neutral. This plan uses whites, grays, and black to build an elegant color palette. Some designers include browns, from cream to chocolate, in this category. The neutral plan needs value, intensity, and textural contrasts to be effective.

In most of these formulas, you need to combine a range of values and intensities to use the colors to full advantage. For instance, in the case of the classic red and green of Christmas, the red is a pure, intense hue, and the green is deeper than the pure hue, darker in value, and lower in intensity.

Color *VARIATIONS*

You don't paint your dining room red; you paint it rouge, crimson, or scarlet. Using descriptive language for colors communicates the intricacies of their characteristics.

Mixing basic colors with one another or with white, black, or gray in varying proportions gives you thousands of options. All colors have three characteristics: hue, intensity, and value. These variations result in producing an endless range of colors.

HUE

Hue is the purest form of a color.

INTENSITY

Intensity describes a color's degree of purity, or saturation. Saturated colors appear more vivid to the eye. You can diminish the intensity of a color by adding either white or black to it; the color becomes paler or grayer depending on how much you add.

VALUE

Value refers to the relative lightness or darkness of a color. As a color is mixed with white, gray, or black, it moves away from its pure color, becoming a tint or a shade.

   A *tint* is a color that has been lightened by the addition of white. The more white you add, the paler the color. For example, pinks are tints of pure red. On the color wheel, tints lie inside the pure hues and move toward the center of the wheel as they get progressively lighter (page 9).

   A *shade* is a color that has been darkened by the addition of black. The more black you add, the darker the color. Forest green is a shade of pure green. Shades lie outside the pure colors on the color wheel (page 9) and move outward as they get darker.

The vivid blue above the window combines with the pale yellow of the walls to display a classic mix of intensities.

Here the colors all come on strong, from the cabinet fronts to the walls to the border around the mirror.

A **tone** is a color that has been modified with gray, creating a more subtle or toned-down version of a color. Mustard is a tone of yellow.

Neutral colors are white, black, and gray, which are blends of white and black. Technically white and black are noncolors because white reflects all the colors in the full visible spectrum, and black absorbs all of them.

Working with different values of various colors in your decorating plan is more pleasing than choosing colors of the same value; it keeps colors from competing with each other. Blue and green, for instance, don't always work well together, but a high-value pastel blue and a low-value dark green can be an effective combination.

The effect of low-value color selections, such as the peach bed ruffle, tablecloth, and pillows, is to create a quiet atmosphere, perfect for a bedroom.

Shades

VALUE

Tints

| Black | 25% Hue 75% Black | 50% Hue 50% Black | 75% Hue 25% Black | Hue | 75% Hue 25% White | 50% Hue 50% White | 25% Hue 75% White | White |

75% Color 25% Gray

50% Color 50% Gray

25% Color 75% Gray

Gray

TONE

Cool TOOL

A color value scale is a handy tool when mixing and matching colors. The value scale is separated into bars ranging from black at one end to white at the other, with the hue (pure color) in the middle. The shades or tints represent the relative darkness or lightness of a color (usually shown as 10 values for convenience on the scale, although the actual range of colors is continuous). The value is controlled by adding or subtracting black or white to the hue. The value scale shows the effect of adding a neutral gray ("gray-dation") to the tints and shades.

Color and EMOTION

You often use color to describe emotion. You say someone is red with anger, green with envy, sad and blue, rosy with optimism—even purple with passion. Research confirms that different colors stimulate emotional and physical reactions in people. When selecting color for a room, keep in mind that each color has a psychological value. Review the following emotional correspondences and strive to make your design feel right as well as look right.

RED

Red is warm, bold, stirring, and energetic. In its pure form it can increase heart rate and raise body temperature. Use red in rooms where activity occurs, like a family room, or where sleeping and resting is not a priority. For a deep, intense setting, use other colors sparingly in a red room. The eye is drawn to red, so it also makes an eye-catching accent color.

YELLOW AND ORANGE

Yellow and orange are just as exciting as red, but they are more cheerful than bold, more bright than stimulating. Yellow and orange warm and enliven any room where they are used but work especially well to brighten dark rooms. On large surfaces they are best used in light values.

GREEN

Green is the dominant color in nature. It is a pleasing, organic, fresh, calming, and restful color. It is a great color for any room where you want a relaxed and fresh atmosphere.

BLUE

Blue, the color of sky and water, creates fresh, cool, and restful feelings. Blue walls can make a south- or west-facing room feel cooler. Because it "recedes," blue also creates the illusion of space and distance, conjuring up emotions of haughtiness, formality, reserve, and sadness. In spite of evoking such contradictory reactions, blue is a favorite because it is easy on the eyes and the nerves, making it an excellent choice for rooms where you want to relax or sleep.

PURPLE

Purple is lush, regal, and passionate. It is an intense and highly emotional color, partly because it straddles the line between the warm red and cool blue. This makes it a difficult color to use in interior design, and it is usually confined to the role of an accent.

BLACK AND WHITE

Black and white are pure contrasts and intensifiers—light and dark, yin and yang, all or nothing. Dramatic and elegant together, they lend sophistication in decor that is stylish and urban.

Color and **LIGHT**

Color comes to your eyes as reflected light. Change the type of light, and you will change the color. You need to control light sources, as well as the paint on a wall, to control color. Here are four types of light that affect color:

Natural light is sunlight (top photo), the purest light and the easiest on the eye. It covers the entire spectrum of light and shows the truest color.

General lighting is also known as ambient lighting. This artificial light can come from incandescent, fluorescent, or halogen sources. "Daylight" bulbs provide a broader spectrum of light than standard bulbs, producing a warmer, more natural effect.

Task lighting highlights a work space or feature area. Track lighting or under-cabinet lighting are examples of this type of light.

Accent or specialty lighting (bottom photo), adds visual interest and drama to your decor. Lamps are common examples of accent lighting.

Creating a COLOR PLAN

Wall Wizards learn how to create a color plan; they are not born with this skill. You can develop a skilled eye by studying how color is used around you. Look at specific hues, values, and intensities. Relate what you see to the color wheel and note the combinations you find particularly pleasing.

Snip 'n' clip

Clip photos of rooms that you like and keep them in a file. Add new clippings and color swatches as you find them. From time to time, weed out those that no longer please you. Eventually you will see a pattern develop that shows which colors you are drawn to and which you dislike.

Go au naturel

Nature is a good source of inspiration for a color plan. Look at the brilliant plumage of birds or the dramatic colors of a seashore sunset. The color combinations found in nature are all pleasing and good models to use for decorating plans.

Museum-hop

View paintings and tapestries in museums and art books. Any classic work of art can be a good inspiration for your design. The works of the Impressionists, such as Manet, Monet, Degas, and Renoir, are especially helpful because they show how colors merge to create other colors when viewed from a distance.

Build a file folder full of items that catch your eye and see what color combinations emerge as your personal favorites.

Tips 'N' TRICKS

Create a "color folder" for each room to document your color plans. Use an expanding pocket folder to archive the swatches, clippings, and samples you use to decorate. Take this portable information tool with you when you shop to guide your purchases.

Train your eyes to recognize the effective use of color by studying art books and decorating magazines. Learn from the wisdom of others.

Read all about it

Read decorating magazines. The articles are excellent resources because the homes displayed are often created by professional interior designers. Advertisements in these magazines can be a source of ideas as well.

Shop 'til you drop

Browse the showrooms in high-quality furniture stores. The displays, arranged by interior designers, emphasize effective color plans in order to sell the store's design services. Model homes and decorator show houses are sources of similar ideas.

Study style

Study decorative fabrics, from Oriental rugs to drapery and upholstery fabrics, and pay attention to fine-quality wallcoverings. You can even borrow books of wallcoverings from home centers or decorating stores to view the designs and colors in your home.

Trash trends

Beware of color trends. When trendsetting designers use certain colors, manufacturers begin making everything from bath towels to picture frames in these hues. Suddenly what seemed new and exciting becomes commonplace and trite. Then the cycle begins again with a new color. To reflect your personal style, choose your favorite colors for walls and major pieces; use the latest trendy colors sparingly.

Color me happy

The most important element in a successful color plan is your own preferences. What colors make you feel happy? What colors are you most often wearing when people compliment you on your appearance? What colors dominate your wardrobe? These are colors you favor naturally, and the best colors for your home.

Cool TOOL

If you can't decide on a color, ask for a color fan deck. This nifty tool shows the exact color combinations a specific manufacturer offers. Use this portable color tool in your home to see how the light in a room influences a particular color. Fan decks at professional paint stores cost about $15 each.

Quiz the Wiz

How can I choose color like a Wall Wizard?

Here are several techniques to help you on your color quest:

☆ For white walls throughout the house, use the same value of white in every room for a unifying effect.

☆ Use differences of scale and proportion to create interest in a room. Using all pale tints in a room can make the colors look weak and dull, using only mid-tones produces monotony, and a plan composed entirely of dark shades will feel gloomy. Combinations, however, create a dynamic and refreshing décor.

☆ When painting each room a different color, paint spaces between the rooms, such as foyers, hallways, and staircases, in grayed-down colors to create transitions.

☆ Pick a color for your home and use it in different amounts in each room. It can be the dominant color in one room, the secondary color in another, an accent in the third, and the color of an accessory in a fourth, for example. This technique will create harmony throughout the house.

The combination of color tones in this bedroom creates a dynamic and refreshing space.

Pastel hues add to the light, expansive feel of this room.

Stopping the wall color below the ceiling lowers the visual height of the room, making it feel more cozy.

- ☆ Light colors are expansive and airy; they make rooms seem larger and brighter. Dark colors are sophisticated and warm; they give large rooms a more intimate appearance.

- ☆ If you want dark or intensely colored walls, tint the primer the same color as the finish coat.

- ☆ Camouflage architectural defects by using neutral paint colors that blend with neutral walls, ceilings, and floors.

- ☆ Carry wall color up to the ceiling to raise the visual height of a room. If there is a crown or cove molding, paint it the same color. A light color also makes the ceiling seem higher.

- ☆ To lower a ceiling or make a room feel cozy, stop the wall color 9 to 12 inches below the ceiling. You can also paint the ceiling a dark color.

- ☆ Make a long, narrow room seem wider by painting the shorter walls a darker color than the longer walls.

- ☆ To coordinate a room, tint white ceiling paint slightly by adding a splash of the wall color.

The dark colors here make the room more intimate. The monochromatic plan uses a variety of textures to add interest.

Why can't my spouse and I agree on color selections?

It's an age-old question with an age-old answer: Men and women see colors differently. Women have more cones (light-sensitive receptor cells) in their eyes, making them more able to distinguish among the slightest variations in colors. Men, on the other hand, have more rods (a different type of receptor cells) in their eyes, making them more responsive to motion but less attuned to color.

Just the *RIGHT AMOUNT* of color

Getting the right amount of color in a room is the most important part of a color plan. It's also the most difficult. In fact, few people feel confident creating a color plan, so they tend to use a favorite color over and over until it loses its impact. Avoid this common mistake by using one of the following methods to create your color plan.

One dominant color

Use one color in its different values and intensities over most of the room, then add its complementary, analogous, triad, or split-complementary colors as accents on smaller furniture pieces, window coverings, accent rugs, and accessories such as pillows. A monochromatic arrangement is another version of this design plan. It uses one color in shades and tints of different values and adds one accent color. The accent color is a contrast of the base color—often its complement.

Blue dominates this room, appearing not only on the walls but also in the glassware and pitcher, on the bowl, and even on the ceramic chicken.

Cool *TOOL*

Paint a piece of white 24×30-inch foam-core board the desired color. When it's dry, you can move the board around the room, testing the paint in a variety of light conditions. Hold it vertically on the walls to view it. This method also lets you see how furniture and accessories in a room look when positioned against or next to a particular color.

When you've selected your color, cut an 8½×11-inch piece from the foam-core board with your final color choice. Keep this sample with you when you shop to make it easier to match items to the paint.

Split colors

This plan requires significant contrast in the values and intensities of colors to be effective. For example, use one color on the walls, the window coverings, and most upholstered furniture. Choose a different color for the floor, and add a third color and variations of the first two for accent furniture and accessories.

Two dominant colors

For this color plan, select one dominant color for the walls, floor, and smaller pieces of furniture and another color for the major pieces of furniture. Because you are working with only two colors, pay special attention to the mix of contrasting values and intensities. Also add texture contrast in the paint or wallcovering or in the upholstery and accessory fabrics.

The doors in this kitchen (above) feature a lighter value color, while the casework provides a darker but complementary color. The living room walls (below) are painted with one strong color; the fireplace offers a second, equally strong selection.

Quiz the Wiz

We painted our kitchen and the color looks awful. What should we do?

Sometimes this happens in spite of the most careful sampling. You have two remedies: Use the existing color as the base and apply a glaze as a decorative effect (see page 145) or repaint the walls. If you repaint, start by coating the surface with a white primer. That way the color underneath won't alter the new color.

Why does the paint on the wall look different from the paint on the sample card?

You probably selected the color by looking at it under a different type or intensity of light than what's in your room. Sunlight, daylight, fluorescent light, halogen light, and incandescent light affect colors differently. So bring the sample card into the room you intend to paint and look at it several times during the day. See how the color looks using different kinds of artificial light before making a final decision. To get an even better idea of what the color will look like in your room, purchase a small quantity of the paint and apply it to a white foam core board, then view the board in several positions in the room you intend to paint (see "Cool Tool" opposite).

Formulas for
SUCCESS

*F*inally you've made your decision; you're going to paint your bedroom pale blue. You have several options to find just the right blue:

Standard factory finish

When you choose a gallon of paint straight off the shelf of your home supply store, you have selected a premixed, standard factory finish. Color selection is limited, but because this paint was manufactured in large batches, there are some advantages: Compared to custom-mixed colors, factory-blended paints are mixed more thoroughly, are more resistant to fading, and are more consistent in color.

Standard-mixed colors

You'll find these colors on the paint chip cards displayed in the store. They are mixed in the store according to the paint company's predetermined formula. Most people use these colors for their painting projects.

Custom-mixed colors

Do you want to match your paint color to the small red flowers in your Oriental rug? Then ask for paint custom-mixed by retail paint dealers, decorating centers, or hardware stores. The dealer can perform a computerized analysis of a color card or fabric swatch to determine a precise color formula. This technology makes it easy to mix virtually any color you choose.

Accent colors

Accent colors are factory-prepared, pure, solid colors such as red, blue, yellow, and black. Mix them with each other to get rich, deep colors. Considered premium coatings, they are very durable and resist fading—useful for a sunny room. Used in small, intense ways, they create more drama.

Specialty paints

One other type of paint is worth mentioning here: specialty paints, such as glazes; crackle, suede, and pebble finishes; Venetian plaster; chalkboard paint; and many others. Once available only to professional painters, now they are offered to do-it-yourselfers.

Paint dealers, decorating centers, and home improvement stores can perform computerized color analysis and custom-mix colors to meet your exact needs.

Decorating PYRAMID

Many people who attend my color workshops ask: Where do I start decorating? My answer is to plan in one direction and work in the opposite direction. Let me explain:

This pyramid illustrates how to create a decorating plan. Start your planning with the least changeable design element in a room and work toward the easiest to change. So rather than starting with the walls, which can be painted a different color every week, build your decorating project literally from the ground up. Consider first the carpet or floor covering. Then move up to the drapes and upholstery, based on the flooring choice you've made. Continue on up the pyramid until you reach paint, the crowning glory of the room.

With your plan complete, it's time to get to work. Start with paint and work your way through the other design elements in the room.

☆ **Paint** – When all other design elements are present, then choose the appropriate color to paint walls.

☆ **Accessories** – Accessories, such as collectibles and displays, add personality and style to a room.

☆ **Lighting** – Some lighting is permanent or fixed; lamp lighting and under-counter lighting can highlight areas and add dimension. Lighting also sets the mood in a room.

☆ **Artwork** – Artwork reflects a sense of style and adds personality to a room.

☆ **Furniture** – Furniture is expensive to replace, but rearranging pieces can give a room a completely different look. The style of furniture creates a particular atmosphere.

☆ **Fabric** – Coordinate fabric for upholstery and drapes with flooring. Fabrics with a design and pattern give you a built-in selection of dominant and accent colors.

☆ **Flooring** – Choose carpeting, wood, vinyl, or linoleum floors first. These are big-ticket items that are expensive and time-consuming to change. A neutral shade gives you the most flexibility in your design plan; whereas a pattern or colorful floor can enliven a room.

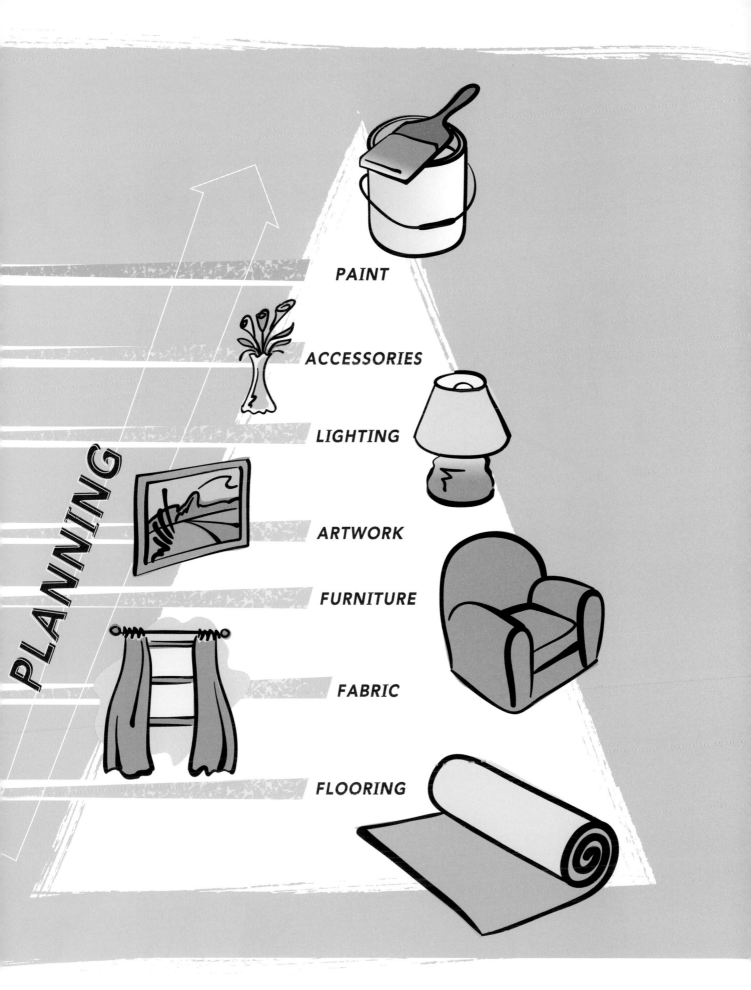

PAINT

ACCESSORIES

LIGHTING

ARTWORK

FURNITURE

FABRIC

FLOORING

PLANNING

All about WALLS

Walls are the best place to begin your paint project. They are the largest surfaces in a room, and how you finish them affects every other aspect of your decorating plan. Yet that doesn't mean walls must dominate your decor. You can decide whether the walls will be a room's backdrop or its focal point.

Background walls

If walls will form the backdrop, choose their color after selecting the room's other major elements. Then pull a coordinating color from one of those sources. The coordinating color can be a shade or tint of a dominant color; a shade or tint of a pattern used in the room's carpet, decorative fabrics, or wallcovering; or a shade or tint drawn from a painting, an important piece of furniture, a fireplace surround, or even a view. It can also be a shade or tint of a color complementary to the dominant color. You probably will find that complement used in one of the patterned fabrics in the room. Choosing a new finish for the walls in this manner works particularly well when you're not planning on changing anything else in the room.

Neutral walls

This method uses a neutral paint color on the walls, making them a backdrop for other elements in the room, such as its architecture, furnishings, or art. It can make good sense not to upstage dominant elements with "look-at-me" walls. Even if you narrow your choices to white, more than 60 variations are available, each with subtle differences in tint, value, intensity, and warmth.

Focal-point walls

If the walls are the most important feature in the room as well as the largest, choose their finish first and then build your decorating plan around them. This method is more difficult than picking a background color because you don't have other color elements to guide your selection. When that's the case, indulge yourself and choose one of your favorite colors. Or decide what mood you want a

In some cases, walls serve as background for other major elements that demand attention, such as a painting.

Furnishings take center stage here, while the walls, painted a neutral color, serve only as backdrop.

The wall color sets the mood for energetic entertaining in this room; the other elements follow.

Painting the pillar the same color as the walls minimizes its impact on this room setting.

room to convey and pick your color accordingly. When mood is your guide, take into account the room's function, architectural style, size, lighting, and view before making your color choice. Decide whether the room should be light or dark, warm or cool. If the room receives minimal light, choose a light wall color—unless, of course, you want the room to be dark and cozy. Make sure the color, texture, and pattern of the wall finish suits the room's architectural style.

Colorful disguise

One more word about color: Besides being an important design element, color has the ability to manipulate what you actually see in a room.

Light colors, subtle textures, and small patterns make a room seem more expansive, so they make ideal choices when you want a small room to appear larger than it is or to emphasize a larger room's spaciousness. To visually raise a low ceiling, consider a strong vertical pattern.

Dark or intense colors; bold, coarse textures; and large patterns shrink a room because they bring the walls close to you. That's desirable in a spacious room, especially if you want a cozy, intimate effect. It's also desirable if you want to emphasize the comfortable snugness of a small room.

Decide whether you want woodwork, moldings, and other architectural features hidden or highlighted. If you want them to disappear, paint them a color that matches the wall to diminish their presence; to make them stand out, paint them a contrasting color.

Wizard WARNING

Wall Wizards like a change of scenery, but as a beginning painter, you should build your skills by applying colors in a private area of your home—a bedroom, bathroom, or laundry room, for example. Even a storage room or garage is a good place to experiment. When you've mastered these spaces, it's much easier to produce professional results in the more visible rooms in your home.

Prep Works

*N*obody wakes up on a Saturday morning and says, "Gee, I think I'd like to prep my living room today." You want to jump in and start painting, thinking you can complete a project in a weekend. But take it from the Wall Wizard: The success of any home improvement project depends on preparation. Eighty percent of the success of any painting project is in the preparation; another 10 percent comes from skills of the painter; the final 10 percent from the materials.

Because paint is a liquid that conforms to a surface, its finish is ultimately only as good as the surface itself. Don't count on paint to cover a dirty, damaged, or discolored surface. Plan to put in one to three hours of prep time for every hour spent painting.

It sounds like a lot of work, but the preparation is the foundation for a quality paint job. The more time you spend properly prepping a surface, the faster and easier the application will go, and the better the quality of finish.

Tools *THAT RULE*

You don't have to spend a lot of money to be a successful painter, but you do need the right equipment. That's why Wall Wizards take the time to gather the appropriate tools and materials before they start projects.

The key word for selecting and handling tools and materials is control. Liquids, for example, are always easier to deal with when wet than when dry. So choose tools that control paint and other liquids in their purest, wettest form. Paper dissolves when it comes into contact with water-based materials; metal rusts. Plastic is a great material; it keeps liquids in their wet state and doesn't interact with them, and forms a barrier to protect you and other surfaces.

RULES OF TOOLS

Invest in the best. This doesn't mean the most expensive; but rather the most effective tools. Here are a few rules to consider when purchasing tools:

☆ Buy quality, not quantity. Quality wears better and lasts longer.

☆ Buy plastic or stainless-steel products; they are unaffected by water-based or oil-based products. Look for nonporous materials; they're easier to clean up.

☆ Buy brightly colored tools. Fluorescent colored tools are easier to locate and make it easier to avoid mishaps.

☆ Buy plastic containers with airtight lids for short- and long-term storage.

☆ Buy tools that hold you, rather than tools that you have to hold. Easy, stress-free handling and use results in better tool control and less muscle fatigue. Look for ergonomic grips built into a tool.

CLEANING TOOLS

Have on hand various sizes of plastic **trash bags** and **resealable plastic bags** for storing hardware and switch plates. For dusty cleanup tasks, a **shop vacuum cleaner,** a **push broom** with **dustpan,** and **dusting brush** will come in handy. You'll need **5-gallon buckets,** clean rinsing **tile sponges,** a sponge head **floor mop** with nylon scrubbing pads, and a nylon bristle **deck brush** with extension pole. Large **household sponges** with a nylon scrubbing pad and 2-quart **plastic buckets,** and lots of **terry-cloth towels** will round out your cleaning supplies.

MAGIC MATERIALS

A solvent is a substance diluted into a liquid and used to dissolve other materials. Solvents are described as cold, warm, or hot according to their degree of volatility, chemical makeup, and use. Your selection of cleaning solutions should be based on the surface and the type of paint with which you're working: water for latex, mineral spirits for oil.

Cold. Water is nature's solvent; liquid fabric softener is a surfactant that makes water wetter. This cold solvent turbocharges water and breaks down the binders and additives in water-based paints. It is people-safe and earth-friendly.

Water-based cleaning products, such as trisodium phosphate (TSP), ammonia, hydrogen peroxide, and all-purpose cleaners remove dirt and are neutralized with distilled white vinegar. These products are people-safe and earth-friendly.

Warm. When a moderate cleaning material is needed, denatured alcohol, acetone, muriatic acid, and rubbing alcohol are all considered warm solvents due to their ability to mix in water or oil solutions. These products are also effective surface cleaners, but be sure to rinse well. They are safe when handled, stored, and disposed of properly.

Hot. The solvent for oil-based paints must be a petroleum-based product. Mineral spirits or paint thinners are hot solvents and are formulated to break down the chemistry of oil-based paints. Naphtha, turpentine, and lacquer thinner are other hot solvents. Be sure to protect yourself and handle these materials with caution. Use, store, and dispose of these hazardous materials properly.

CLEANING CHEMICALS

Wear heavy-duty gloves and eye protection for safety. Trisodium phosphate, known as **TSP**, is an alkaline cleaner that dissolves grease and deglosses surfaces. To kill mold and mildew, use **hydrogen peroxide.** Use an ammonia-based or an alkaline household cleaner for removing dirt and as a mild acid rinsing agent white vinegar. As base material, **baking soda** is used to create or neutralize chemical reactions. **Muriatic acid** is used to clean masonry. Look for a water-soluble paint cleaner that removes paint from rugs, floors, and woodwork. **Citrus-based cleaners,** such as Goof Off 2, work especially well. **Rubbing alcohol** can clean grease, grime, dirt, fly boogers, spider snot, and other organic spots from metal hardware. When working with volatile chemicals, use only **nonflammable shop rags** that are specially coated to prevent spontaneous combustion.

PROTECTIVE CLOTHING

Start with the most important tool: you. Never come into contact with paints, stains, or solvents. Why? Because your body is a giant sponge, and you can absorb these chemicals through your skin. To protect yourself, wear **nonporous vinyl gloves.** Latex gloves tear easily and are porous, allowing paint to seep through. Sprinkle **baby powder** into the gloves so they slip on more easily. Wrap a piece of masking tape around the cuff to seal it. To protect bare arms, spray on some **nonstick cooking oil.** It will prevent water-based paint from penetrating your skin. I figure if you can eat it, you can wear it!

For full-body protection, put on **disposable paper coveralls** and **painter's hat** or **shower cap.** (**Bowl covers** make great head-protection gear, and they're good for popping over paint buckets to keep the paint from drying out if you pause for a minute during painting.) Wear **goggles,** safety glasses, or a face shield to protect your eyes from dust, chips, or paint; a **dust mask** filters out dust; a **respirator** protects you from dust and chemical fumes.

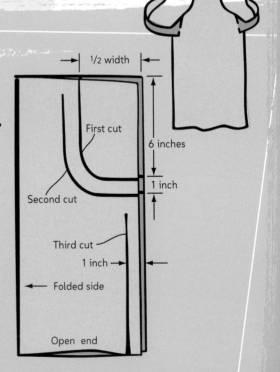

✦ *Cool TOOL*

It sounds obvious, but anything you don't want to get paint on, including yourself, should be covered. That's why I invented the trash bag apron. It's inexpensive, easy to make, and keeps you clean. Lay out a 13-gallon tall kitchen plastic trash bag (a trash compactor bag works best) with the sealed end at the top and open end down. Fold it in half lengthwise. Opposite the folded edge, use scissors to cut off the top corner in an arcing cut to make the armholes (first cut). Make the second cut to create the neck straps, starting about 1 inch below the sealed top edge, cutting parallel about 1 inch in from the first cut. The third cut forms the waist ties. Tie the neck straps together. Be sure to save the pouches created by the first cut; you can use them to store a paint can lid.

1/2 width

First cut

Second cut

6 inches

1 inch

Third cut

1 inch

Folded side

Open end

PROTECT THE ROOM

Everyone thinks of 2-inch-wide masking tape when it's time for painting. But that beige-colored tape has adhesive that is so sticky, it can sometimes rip the paint and wallcovering right off your woodwork and walls. One of the best things to happen for painters is the development of different types of **masking tapes** designed to perform best with various types of paint. **Blue tape** is designed for latex paints and other water-based finishes. **Purple tape** is for oil-based finishes. **Green tape** is for lacquers. All three stay on regardless of rain and humidity and stick for at least seven days. But the real benefit of these new, colored masking tapes is that they pull off any surface—even paint or wallcovering—without causing damage. Think of colored tape as an insurance policy that protects you from messy mistakes.

Pretaped **masking film** is Wizard thinking at its best. This inexpensive tool has a built-in cutter and is designed to easily dispense a replaceable roll of masking tape and plastic sheeting. The film unfolds to about 24 inches, providing a drop cloth that protects surrounding surfaces from spills and splatters. The film clings to a surface so it won't flip up into a freshly painted surface, and it is biodegradable, so you can throw it away with the trash. Use **lip balm** to mask glass panes when painting window trim.

Why invest in a big, heavy tarp like the pros use when you'll only use it five times in your life? Instead purchase a **disposable paper/plastic drop cloth**. Face the paper side up to absorb, the plastic side down to protect a surface. This product is nonslip so you won't go sliding across it, and it is biodegradable, so you can wad it up and toss it in the trash when you are finished.

For protecting furniture and other items that are too big to move, use **9×12-foot, .7-mil plastic sheeting**

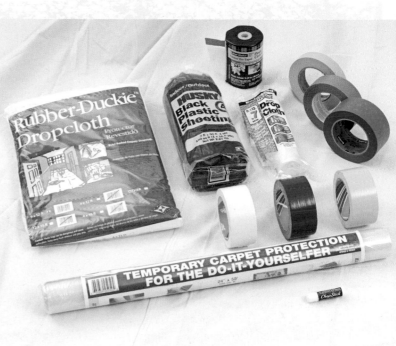

because it provides a lot of coverage. It is inexpensive and biodegradable, so you can throw it away when you're finished. It does have one drawback: it is hard to unfold. Here's a **Wall Wizard trick:** Take the plastic, still in the package, and place it in the freezer for about 30 minutes. This removes the static charge on the plastic, so when you take it out, it's easy to unfold. If you immediately lay it out over furniture, it will wrap itself around the furniture as it warms up. One more tip: Don't use old bedsheets or newspapers when you paint. The paint will go right through them, staining the surface beneath.

Painting from the PANTRY

Who knew something as simple as plastic wrap could create magic? Use it to cover doorknobs and keep speckles and splatters off hardware. Do the same with cordless phones. If you are painting the ceiling, press a sheet of plastic wrap over your eyeglasses. You can still see through them, but the wrap protects the lenses from paint drops.

CAULKING AND PATCHING

A **5-in-1 tool** has a point for digging out old caulking or opening cracks on plaster, a scraper head for removing wallpaper and old paint, a putty knife edge for filling nail holes in wallboard or plaster with spackle, a curved edge for cleaning paint from a roller, and a hard, flat end on the handle to drive popped nails back into the wall. You can even pry open paint can lids with the flat end and use the pointed end to punch holes in the lid rim. A **2-inch putty knife** will prove useful during preparation.

Interior and exterior **surfacing compound, wallboard joint compound,** or patching plaster will fill holes and cracks in the walls; use **6-inch and 10-inch broad knives** to smooth patching compound. **Caulking in a pressurized can** is handy for filling gaps between woodwork and walls. You'll need a dripless **caulking gun** and tubes of **white, water-based acrylic caulk** to fill larger gaps and cracks, and a damp sponge to smooth the caulk.

Home centers sell a number of **ready-to-use patching compounds** in handy dispensers. One of my favorites is Patch Stick. It dispenses with a simple turn; its cap forms a flat scraper; the lid is airtight. Caulking is also available in pressurized containers, such as Easy Caulk. Another handy product is Goodbye Cracks, a silicon latex spray that fills in cracks in walls, creating a flexible bonding surface.

Use **wood filling compound** for holes in moldings. Brightly colored **toothpicks** come in handy for marking screw holes that you'll want to find after painting.

SANDING

A variety of **sandpaper sheets** with grits from 60–400 is necessary to properly sand surfaces. A **sanding block** to smooth a patching job, along with a **palm sander** or half-sheet orbital sander, work nicely as well. A pivoting **drywall sander** uses a nonclogging abrasive screen rather than sandpaper, and it has an extension pole for high or hard-to-reach places. Some pole sanders can be hooked to a shop vacuum, which sucks up the dust before it can escape into the air. If heavy sanding is required, wear a particle **dust mask** and place a **box fan** in a window to blow the dust out. Never use wet tools to remove dust; the water will turn the dust to mud and coat the surface. A sticky **tack rag** picks up fine dust between coats of paint. **Tile sponges** and **nylon scrubbing pads** are used for wet-sanding.

WALLCOVERING REMOVAL

Removing wallcovering requires a few tools. Use a broom handle to roll strippable wallcoverings off the wall. A **rolling mop bucket** eliminates the need for you to repeatedly bend over and move it (or place a bucket on a planter dolly). A 3-gallon plastic **pump sprayer** quickly applies wallpaper remover to large areas; use a **trigger-handle spray bottle** for smaller areas. Buy a new sprayer; don't use one that has been used for herbicides or pesticides. A **Paper Tiger**® is a handy tool that perforates wallpaper and makes it easier to remove. A **paper scraper** has a wide, flat edge that is angled so it easily lifts wallpaper from the surface. Never substitute a broad knife for a paper scraper.

You will also need **baking soda, fabric softener,** and **wallpaper remover concentrate** with enzymes to make the potion for wallpaper removal. Stir 1 cup of **vinegar** into 1 gallon of water to rinse walls. Have several clean 5-gallon buckets on hand. Have plenty of **.7-mil plastic sheeting** to cover the walls from top to bottom.

WALL REPAIR

You will need **fiberglass mesh reinforcing tape** and **quick-drying plaster compound** for medium-size holes. For large holes, have a **drywall saw,** scraps of drywall, paper joint tape, oil-based sealer, and **wallboard screws** on hand. To drive the fasteners, you'll want a corded or cordless **drill driver** (cordless models are more convenient). You'll also need a **tape measure**, a **utility knife,** and a **drywall square** or **carpenter's square** to measure and cut the drywall.

Filling materials include all-purpose joint compound, plaster patching, and quickset patching mud. For convenience in mixing large buckets of joint compound, chuck a **mixing auger** into your drill. Several sizes of **taping knives** smooth the drywall compound after your patch is applied. Carry material in a mudding tray. **Slotted-head** and **phillips screwdrivers** come in handy for opening containers and snugging down drywall screws; a **hammer** and **ring-shank drywall nails** are used to hang sheets.

Painting from the PANTRY

Here's a $2 Wall Wizard solution for cleanup: baby wipes. Think about it: These wipes are designed to clean up really big messes. The alcohol in the wipes removes any grease, grime, and dirt; the lanolin renders them nonflammable. They're biodegradable; plus they smell better than dirty old rags.

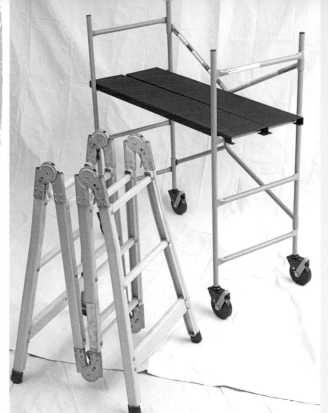

EXTEND YOUR REACH

The **multiladder** is a sturdy, lightweight, and practical home improvement tool. One handy size extends 16 feet long when fully extended, and is composed of four, 4-foot-long sections with multiposition locking hinges between each section. It can be configured as an extension ladder or as a stepladder. You can also create a level work platform on uneven surfaces, such as a stairway or ramp. And here's a great Wizard Trick: Configure the middle two sections horizontally and the end sections down for legs. Place a sheet of plywood on top of the multiladder and you have a work table.

If you have a high ceiling or stairwell, you might need **scaffolding**. You can rent scaffolding from most equipment rental outlets. The easiest type to use has locking wheels and folds for transport or storage. Look for the type that is narrow enough to roll through a standard doorway.

5-foot platform ladder

This lightweight ladder is my choice for giving you a step up in the world. Its sturdy yet simple design allows you to directly face the wall while you work. It weighs only 10 pounds, so you can easily close it with one hand by lifting up the built-in shelf, and it also folds 3 inches flat for storage. When opened it has two steps: The upper one is a 12×18-inch platform, which is easier to stand on than a standard ladder rung and brings you comfortably within reach of an 8-foot ceiling. The ladder has a built-in safety cage, and it is wide enough to bridge over a toilet but narrow enough to place into a bathtub.

Tips 'N' TRICKS

Add peel-and-stick traction strips, available at most hardware and home center stores, to each step of the platform ladder to keep your feet from sliding off. (You can put the same strips on the steps of a multiladder, too.) Put white rubber cane tips, available in hardware stores and pharmacies, on the bottoms of the legs for better stability and so the ladder won't scuff or scratch surfaces, such as floors or bathtubs.

Ready the ROOM

You've probably tried to paint around furniture and carpeting, but it always happens: You dribble or spill paint on something. That's why step one in prep work is to clear out the room. An empty room is an easy room to paint, so begin by removing everything that you can from the room. Gather anything that is left to one side of the room, away from your work area.

Next disassemble the room. First turn off the power to any outlets or fixtures on the surfaces you will be painting. Then remove all light fixtures, switch and outlet plates, heat registers, and towel rods—anything you will have to paint around. This includes drapes (get them cleaned while they are down) and drapery hardware. Don't try to paint around the hardware; it is too frustrating and time-consuming. Just pay particular attention to how your window treatments are attached and make a diagram, if necessary, so you can reinstall them correctly and without guesswork.

Loosen the canopy or trim piece of a ceiling fixture or chandelier and slide it down the fixture away from the ceiling. Wrap it with plastic trash bags or plastic wrap. Never unscrew a fixture from the electrical box and allow it to hang by its

Painting from the PANTRY

Colored party toothpicks make it a snap to remount drapery hardware, towel bars, or picture hooks in a room. Pack toothpicks snugly into each hole you want to reuse. Then spackle the holes without picks. The toothpicks make the holes easy to find when it's time to reattach the hardware. To help you fasten the hardware securely, snap off the exposed toothpicks, leaving the rest of the toothpicks inside so the screws will seat firmly into the wall.

wires. The wires aren't meant to hold a fixture's weight; there's the immediate danger of falling glass fixtures, as well as the risk that the wires could be damaged, creating an electrical short and a fire hazard later. A ceiling fan is impossible to paint around, so take it down.

Remove switchplates and outlet plates, and protect the switches and outlets themselves with blue masking tape to shield them from paint and moisture.

Place a work table in another room, or outside if you will be using solvents for oil-base paints. You can make a table by laying a piece of plywood or a flush wooden door over two sawhorses.

Starting thinking now: Cleanup is not what you do at the end of the job, it's what you do throughout your project. Place a large, lined trash can in the room to throw away debris as you work. A messy workplace is unsafe and can slow you down.

Tips 'N' TRICKS

I used to have a bad habit of laying switch plates on the floor and losing them under the drop cloth, until I heard "crunch!" Then my wife came up with a brilliant use for resealable storage bags. As you disassemble the room, drop all the switch plates into one medium plastic bag. Remount screws back into their fixtures so they don't get lost or scratch the plastic plates. Separate the hardware for each window, door, and curtain into its own bag and mark its location in the room. Once all the hardware has been bagged and tagged, place the bags into one large bag with the room name on it. For safe keeping, stick the bag on the windowpane of the room with blue tape.

WOOD Work

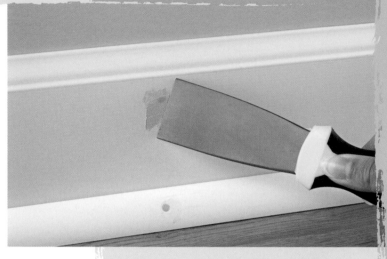

Woodwork, especially baseboards, takes a beating from daily wear and tear. To restore it, begin by patching small holes, such as nail holes, with an interior patching compound.

Sand the patched areas smooth using 180-grit paper, then lightly sand the entire surface. Vacuum the woodwork, then wipe it with a tack cloth to remove dust. Seal the entire surface and paint it.

If the woodwork has sustained extensive damage and the moldings have stock profiles, it is probably easier and faster simply to remove the damaged woodwork and replace it with new molding. Use a small prybar to loosen the molding; place a scrap piece of wood behind the prybar for better leverage and to prevent damage to pieces you might want to save. Use pliers to remove nails; it's usually easier to pull them through the pieces, rather than trying to hammer them back out.

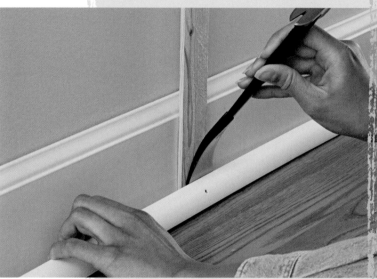

If the woodwork is clear-finished rather than painted, fill holes and defects with a matching wood filler or stainable latex wood putty. Before staining, apply a sanding sealer. The sealer helps better match the stain that you are applying to the existing stain. Then stain the patched areas for trim that will receive a clear finish. After staining apply two thin coats of clear finish.

If the moldings in your house are antique or custom-milled, you'll need to have them professionally restored or have new moldings custom-milled. In that case, consult a professional finish carpenter.

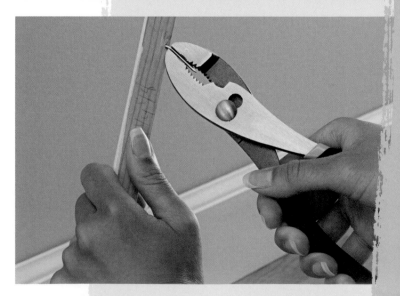

PATCH *Work*

CAULKING

Caulking is one of the faster and easier repair jobs. Using a dripless caulking gun and latex caulk, fill any gaps caused by waviness between the walls and trim. After applying about 8 feet of wet caulking, use a slightly dampened sponge to smooth the bead into the gaps and clean up any excess caulk. Allow it to dry overnight.

PATCHING HOLES

A Wall Wizard finish begins with a smooth surface. To patch a small hole, such as a nail hole, use surfacing compound or drywall joint compound for drywall or plaster. Press the filler into the hole with a putty knife but don't overfill. Several thin coats are better than a thick one.

To patch dents and holes 1–4 inches across in plaster or drywall, put fiberglass-mesh reinforcing tape over the hole, then apply two coats of quick-drying plaster compound over the patch. Let the compound dry between coats. Sand lightly between coats and seal.

Wizard WARNING

Heard the one about using toothpaste to fill holes in the wall? Here's the real story: Toothpaste doesn't hold up over time, and the color sparkles or bleaches can show through the paint. Keep the toothpaste in the bathroom cabinet; use surfacing compound on the walls.

I've seen this happen in old and new houses alike: As the drywall settles, it develops noticeable cracks and opens joints, especially at stress points. Movement can also cause nail heads to pop up. Here are several easy, step-by-step methods to fix drywall problems.

POPPED NAILHEADS

1. Drive a 1½-inch wallboard screw into the stud or joist about 2 inches from the popped nail, so the head is slightly recessed. The screw should pull the wallboard tight against the framing.

2. Drive the popped nail down into the drywall, using a hammer or the handle of a 5-in-1 tool. Resetting the nail should leave a slight dent in the wall. If the nail has worked loose, remove it.

3. With a 6-inch broad knife, cover the nail hole and screw head with lightweight compound. Let it dry overnight, then lightly wet-sand. Apply a thin second coat and let it dry overnight.

4. Apply two coats of white-pigmented sealer, such as Kilz, to seal the porous surfacing compound. The sealer also keeps the paint sheen consistent, promotes proper adhesion for paint, and keeps color variations from showing through the paint.

FILLING CRACKS AND OPEN JOINTS

Stress-point cracks are hard to repair permanently because they can reappear when the house shifts. The secret to filling such cracks is using a rubberized material, such as Goodbye Cracks, that dries flexible. When the crack expands and contracts, the interior vinyl surfacing paste will move with it rather than cracking.

1. If the crack is more than a hairline fissure but narrower than ¼ inch, widen it slightly and undercut its sides with a utility knife. Vacuum, sponge, or brush out the crack to remove all loose debris.

2. Fill the open crack with compound. Strengthen the wet patching material along its entire length with self-adhesive fiberglass mesh tape or moistened paper joint tape. Apply more of the surfacing compound over the tape and level with a broadknife. Let it dry overnight.

3. With a 6-inch broad knife, apply interior vinyl surfacing compound using horizontal and vertical sweeps and let dry. Sand with 120-grit sandpaper. If necessary, apply a third coat with a wider knife.

4. Wet-sand the patch and allow it to dry. Seal the repair with two coats of white-pigmented sealer.

Painting from the PANTRY

When patching white walls and moldings, mix two drops of red food coloring into every 6 ounces of patching compound to make it easy to spot repairs for sanding later.

Repairing **DRYWALL**

Need to repair a large hole? You deserve a Wizard's wand just for tackling the project! Large holes require a bit more patience and care to fix. Follow these directions and you'll do fine.

1. Measure the hole. Cut a piece of drywall large enough to cover it. Trace around the patch onto the wall, and with a drywall saw, cut out the marked area. If the patch is large enough to extend from one stud to another, cut the opening to the center of each stud so you'll have nailing surfaces for the patch.

2. Cut one or more strips of plywood, 1× boards, or drywall scraps. They should be 3 to 4 inches longer than the hole. Slip them behind the opening.

3. Secure the strips to the wall with 1-inch wallboard screws.

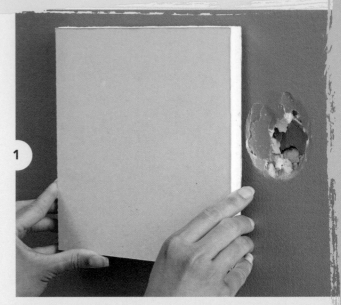

4. Apply strips of fiberglass mesh or moistened paper joint tape over the seams, overlapping the tape at the corners of the patch. Work a thin layer of joint compound into and over the tape, making horizontal and vertical sweeps. Let the patch dry overnight.

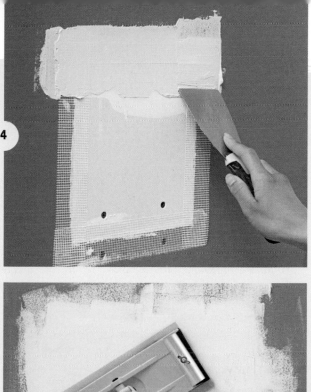

5. Sand level with 120-grit sandpaper. Skim a second coat of compound over the entire patch, feathering it out slightly farther than the first coat. Let the patch dry completely.

6. Sand with 120-grit sandpaper and seal with white-pigmented, oil-based sealer.

DRY SANDING

Sanding is the key to a flawless finish. The goal of sanding is to create a rough surface or tooth for material to grip, to level filling materials, and to smooth surfaces. The higher the grit number (400), the finer the grit; the lower the number (60), the larger the grit and the greater its abrasive quality. Change sandpaper sheets frequently.

In most situations, light dry-sanding will be enough to remove peaks of patching material and polish the surface. A wallboard sanding screen, handheld sanding block, or power sander works well for large jobs. Don't use a belt sander; it will abrade the surface too much.

Sand drywall and plaster along the longest direction; sand wood with the grain. Before you begin sanding, mask floors and furnishings with plastic sheeting and seal off any major openings from room to room to keep dust from spreading. Keep dust down by placing a box fan in a window, front side facing out, to blow the fine dust out of the room, reducing the amount of cleaning. Wear a respirator and eye protection to reduce your exposure to the dust.

Repairing *PLASTER*

When it comes to making repairs, a Wall Wizard knows when to call in reinforcements. If you have extensive damage to plaster areas larger than 12 inches square, have a professional plasterer do the work. For smaller cracks and holes, do it yourself by cleaning out the crack with a utility knife, then filling it with surfacing compound. Sand smooth.

REINFORCING LOOSE PLASTER

This repair sounds harder than it really is. When plaster is sound but sagging away from the underlying lath, you can repair it by screwing it to the lath.

1. Thread a plaster washer onto a 1½-inch drywall screw. Drive the screw through the plaster into the lath using a power drill-driver. Drive the screw in until the washer is drawn into the plaster surface. To cover the area, space the screws 4 inches apart and drive them into studs or joists whenever possible.

2. Cover the washers with surfacing compound and let it dry.

3. Sand the area with 120-grit sandpaper. Sand the patches flush with the wall. Apply a second coat and let it dry.

4. Sand the patches flush with the ceiling or wall. Seal the repaired area with white-pigmented shellac.

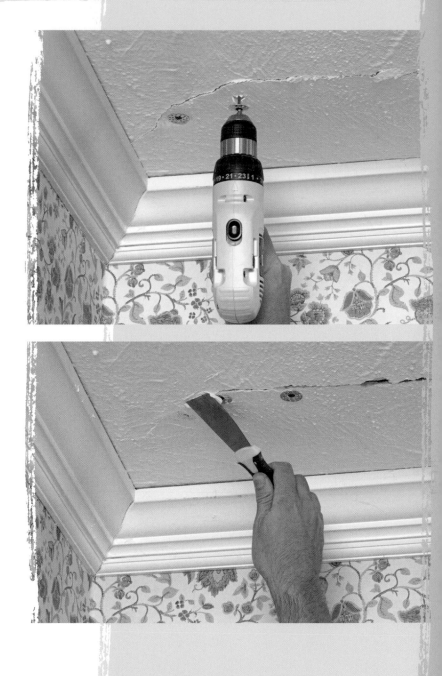

REPAIRING SMALL HOLES IN PLASTER

1. Remove loose material with a putty knife or chisel. Dust the area with a dusting brush. Dampen the edges of the plaster with a commercial latex bonding agent; mix and apply it according to the manufacturer's instructions.

2. Mix patching plaster according to the manufacturer's instructions. Apply the plaster with a broad knife. If the hole is less than ⅛ inch deep, one coat should be enough for good coverage. If the hole is deeper, apply a base coat of plaster in the hole to within ⅛ inch of the surface. Press the plaster into the lath. Let this coat set for 15 minutes, then score the surface with a nail to provide tooth for the next layer. Let the base dry overnight.

3. Apply a second layer of patching plaster, bringing it almost to the surface. Let this layer set for 1–2 hours to harden.

4. Add water to bring the patching plaster to a creamy consistency for the finish coat. Apply the finish coat as smoothly as possible. Make the patched area flush with the surrounding surface. Let the finish coat set for 30 minutes to an hour.

5. Smooth the patch with a damp sponge, blending it into the surrounding surface. This will reduce the amount of sanding necessary. Let the plaster harden.

6. Apply the texture coat to replicate the existing surfaces. Blot the patch with a damp sponge, matching it to the surrounding surface. Let the plaster harden.

7. Lightly sand and seal the area with white-pigmented shellac.

Repairing *CONCRETE*

Latex masonry paints are quite thick, so they easily fill small flaws such as hairline cracks found in bricks, concrete, and other masonry surfaces. To repair larger cracks and chips, follow these simple steps:

1. Dig out any loose material with a stiff wire brush and dust the crack or hole with a clean brush.

2. Wet the area with a spray bottle and let the water soak in for a few minutes.

3. Using a trowel and jointing tool, fill the crack with cement or mortar. Wet the repaired area and let it cure for two weeks before priming or painting.

Repairing BRICK

***C**racks in mortar joints are the most common problem with brick walls. They are often caused by settling and will reappear until the movement stops.*

To repair cracks in a brick wall, follow steps similar to those for concrete block repair: Clean the crack, force mortar into the crack, and tool the joint.

If the surface of the brick is flaking off, the best solution is to cover the area with a skim coat of mortar mix fortified with portland cement.

Clean the brick surface thoroughly with TSP solution and allow it to dry. Apply latex primer formulated for brick using a large, stiff-bristle brush or sponge roller. Use latex masonry paint for the finish coat.

Smoothing TEXTURED WALLS

*O*ne of the questions I'm asked most often in workshops is how to smooth a textured surface. My answer? You've got three choices: sand the texture off, fill the texture in with drywall compound, or cover it up with new drywall. My recommendation? Cover it. It's usually faster, easier, and cleaner. Here are the first two methods; look on page 54 for how to hang new drywall.

To sand the texture from a wall, use a pole sander. You may want to rent a dustless drywall sander; it uses a vacuum attachment to collect all the dust you'll create. Resist the temptation to use a power sander, especially a belt sander. It will dig through the texture too quickly, gouging the wall and leaving an uneven surface.

Here's how to fill in over the texture, known as floating or mudding.

1. Clear out and clean up the room, including the walls. (See "Ready the Room," page 40).

2. Lightly sand the entire wall with a pole sander and a 120-grit sanding screen to knock down any roughness or high peaks on the wall. Do not scrape textured surfaces.

3. Dust the walls with a clean broom or vacuum.

4. If the wall contains any damaged areas, spot-seal them by applying two coats of white-pigmented, oil-based sealer to the wall. Use a disposable brush or a roller with a disposable cover. Let dry, which takes 45 minutes to 1 hour. Sand lightly with a 120-grit sanding screen.

5. Thin premixed joint compound with water in a 5-gallon bucket until it is the

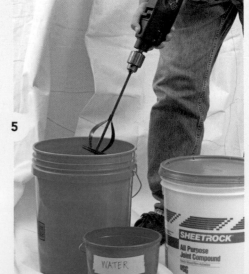

consistency of creamy peanut butter. Mix thoroughly using a drill equipped with a drywall auger, a propeller-type mixing tool. Don't use a mixer designed for paint; it won't adequately stir the compound, which is considerably thicker than paint.

6. Before applying compound, divide the wall into 4-foot-square sections. Scoop the compound into a tray. Start in a corner at the bottom. Apply joint compound to the first 4×4-foot section with a 10-inch broad knife, using broad, horizontal strokes. Then stroke the broadknife vertically in overlapping swaths. Work in one direction, repeating the process on each adjoining section until the lower half of the wall is covered. Return to the starting edge of the wall and float the top half of the wall in the same way. Let the compound dry overnight.

7. Lightly sand the wall, then apply another thin layer of compound for a smooth surface. Apply an oil-based sealer after wet-sanding.

Quiz the Wiz

What can I do about that awful paneling in my living room?

My advice is to install ¼-inch drywall over the paneling to gain a clean, fresh surface (see page 54). If you do want to paint or paper over paneling, you must thoroughly prepare it or you'll end up with a bigger decorating disaster than when you started. Fill, sand, and prime; or cover the paneling with special liner paper.

Installing *NEW DRYWALL*

The best and in many ways easiest coverup for textured walls or paneling is to install new ¼- or ⅜-inch drywall over them.

Drywall sheets are 4 feet wide and commonly available in lengths of 8 or 10 feet (⅜ inch can also be found in 12 or 14-foot sizes). Measure your wall and determine the size of the sheets and their arrangement on the wall (horizontal or vertical) to create the fewest seams and partial sheets possible. Don't place new seams directly over old seams.

Moisture resistant drywall panels are good for use in kitchens or bathrooms. Use drywall screws or ring-shank nails to secure the sheets in place. If you are attaching directly to old gypsum wallboard, use Type G screws. You can also use construction adhesive and fasteners to hold up the new panels.

Remove all the woodwork from the surface, both at the top and the bottom of the walls. Mark the location of all the wall studs so you can easily find them as you install the new drywall sheets. Place a light pencil mark on the ceiling at the point of each stud. Mark the locations of electrical boxes.

Use a utility knife to cut through the outside face of drywall and into the gypsum. Guide the cut with a drywall T-square or a carpenter's square. Make two or three passes to deepen the cut; you don't have to cut all the way through. To complete the cut, hold the sheet and bump the back side with your knee to snap the gypsum. Slice the paper back with a knife.

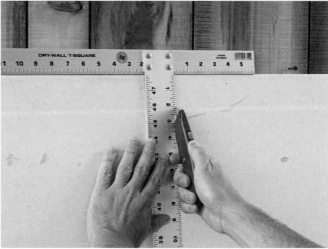

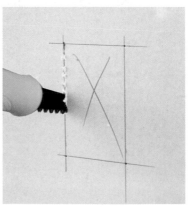

Cut holes for electrical boxes using a drywall saw. Its point can poke through drywall to start the cut, but you can drill holes at the corners of the cutout to make it a little easier. You may need to use box extenders to bring the edge of the switch box flush with the new wall surface.

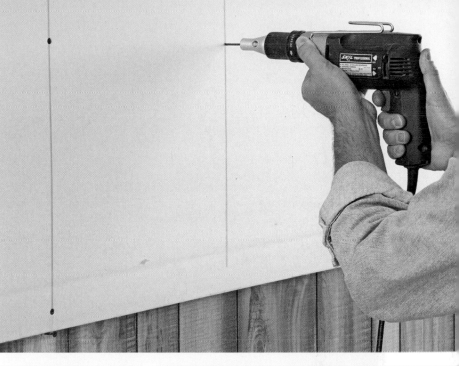

Just before you start hanging a sheet, run a heavy bead of caulk around the top and corners of the wall. This step secures the edges of the drywall and fills any air pockets around the perimeter of the sheet.

With a helper, lift each sheet in place. Handle the sheets carefully; they are heavy and awkward and can break. Drive screws or nails through the sheet into the wall studs. Begin in the center of a panel and work outward. Space nails or screws about 12 inches apart.

Set screw or nail heads just below the surface of the panel, creating a slight dimple, but do not break through the paper facing. If a screw head does break through the paper, place another screw right next to it.

To finish the wall, start by filling screw or nail dimples with joint compound, using a 6-inch broad knife. Cover the joints with self-adhesive fiberglass mesh tape; then cover the tape with a coat of drywall compound. Let the first coat dry 24 hours, scrap off ridges and globs, and apply a second coat with a 10-inch knife. Let it dry and apply a third coat, feathering out the edges of the compound. Smooth the surface by sponging or sanding. Sanding creates lots of dust; be sure to wear a mask and eye protection.

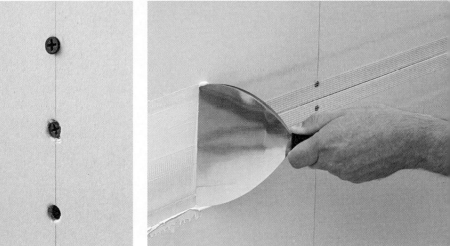

Tips 'N' TRICKS

To mark the location of electrical boxes, drive 2- or 3-inch finishing nails into the studs near the top and bottom of the box. Allow the nailheads to protrude about 1 inch above the surface. Position the new sheet of drywall and press it against the wall. The protruding nail heads will indent the back side of the new drywall and mark placement for the cutouts for the switch boxes.

Quiz the **Wiz**

Am I stuck with textured ceilings or is there hope for being able to smooth them out?

A textured ceiling, especially one that was sprayed before 1970, could contain asbestos. If you are not sure whether asbestos is present, assume it is until a test proves otherwise. There are two ways to smooth a ceiling: scrape it off or cover it up.

Scrape it off

This procedure will make a big mess, so cover the floor completely with taped-down plastic before you start. Remove nonasbestos texturing by soaking it with a solution of 1 cup of ammonia and 1 cup of fabric softener added to 1 gallon of water. Apply the solution with a pump sprayer and let it soak in for about 15 minutes. Reapply the solution as needed to dampen but not soak the texture.

Scrape the softened texture off the ceiling with a floor squeegee. Allow the ceiling to dry and lightly sand the surface. Smooth out any damage with joint compound, seal with oil-based product, and paint.

Cover it up

This method produces the smoothest surface, creates less mess, and avoids disturbing any asbestos-containing material. Begin by stapling 2-mil. plastic over the ceiling to trap and seal the texture.

If you are installing more than a half-dozen ceiling panels, consider renting a wallboard jack. This device raises or lowers a full sheet of wallboard with a simple crank. It has wheels to position the wallboard easily.

If you have just a few wallboard sheets to hang, you can use a T-brace. While it's a bit more cumbersome to use than a wallboard jack, you can make one yourself for a couple dollars, and it will save you two trips to the rental store. Cut one 2×4 about 40 inches long. Cut another piece with a length equal to the distance from the floor to the ceiling of the room you are working in, minus the thickness of the wallboard you're installing, plus one inch. Fasten the two securely together at right angles. (Add angled braces for extra strength and stability.) Hold the brace so the crossmember of the T is near the ceiling, with the T's leg resting on the floor at an angle. Position a sheet of drywall across the T, then move the leg of the brace toward the vertical until the T's crossmember holds the wallboard snug against the ceiling.

Before installation, use a stud finder to locate the ceiling joists. Mark the location of each joist on the top of an adjacent wall with a light pencil mark, so you'll know where to place fasteners when installing the ceiling panels. Install panels parallel to joists. If possible, use panels long enough to span wall to wall.

Lift each panel into place and attach it through the existing ceiling surface and into the joists with 1¾-inch type W wallboard screws using a drill-driver.

Finish by filling screw holes, taping seams, and sanding.

Cool TOOL

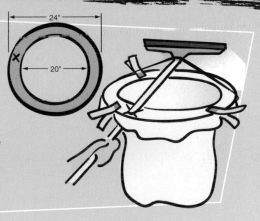

A clever way to dispose of old popcorn ceilings is to scrape the texture material directly into a homemade catch-bag. Cut a 20-inch-diameter circle in the center of a 24-inch-diameter plastic trash can lid. On the remaining plastic rim, cut an X into the plastic. Insert the long handle of a squeegee into the X; wrap a piece of wire around the handle end and attach the ends to the lid. Attach a 13-gallon plastic trash bag over the center hole; secure it with standard spring clips. When you scrape the squeegee across the ceiling, the popcorn will drop into the bag, eliminating much of the mess.

Goodbye to **OLD PAINT**

If the paint job you want to cover is in good condition, it might require nothing more than a good cleaning and a bit of scraping or patching. But if the paint is chipping and peeling, especially on woodwork, you're better off stripping the old paint down to the wood. This is also true if the area is damaged or if you are going to change to a different finish, such as latex instead of oil-based paint.

Chemical paint removers can handle several layers of stubborn paint in one application. Fortunately several new products on the market make this technique faster, easier, and safer than it was 10 years ago. Still, be sure to protect yourself while working: Wear safety goggles, latex gloves, long sleeves, and a dust mask or respirator. Check for lead paint before beginning work (see page 60).

The least aggressive and easiest product to work with is a water-and-citrus-based stripper that is nontoxic, low-odor, and environmentally friendly. It works well but it takes a lot more time to be effective, and it can raise the grain of the wood. This might require additionally sanding and prepping.

When a water-based alkaline or lye-based stripper, such as Peel-Away, is applied, it forms a rubbery coating over the surface. As the material begins to set up, embed the mesh cloth that comes in the kit. When these warm strippers have finished acting on the surface, you can peel

away the stripper, and the old surface comes off with it. These strippers are less messy to use and can remove multiple layers of paint.

Oil- or solvent-based strippers are hot strippers. This means you should have no direct contact with these chemicals because they are petroleum-based. Plus you need to ventilate well because of the fumes. These strippers are flammable, volatile, and environmentally damaging, but they work quickly and thoroughly, and do not raise the grain of wood as much as water-based products.

Wizard **WARNING**

In the cauldron of chemicals, paint strippers are among the most caustic. Take extra precautions to create a strong barrier against these chemicals. First, put on a pair of surgical gloves, then wet your gloved hands with water or rub on a light coat of petroleum jelly. Slip a second pair of gloves over the first. Follow the paint remover manufacturer's directions for use and always work in a well-ventilated area.

To remove paint with a chemical stripper, follow these steps:

1. Working in 1-foot-square sections and using a disposable paintbrush, brush a thick coat of stripper in one direction over the painted surface. Do not brush back and forth—this will reduce the chemical's effectiveness. Let the stripper stand for the recommended time, plus 10 minutes, allowing the paint to soften so it can be easily removed. Apply another coat if the first one dries out.

2. Gently scrape away as much of the softened paint as possible with a coarse abrasive pad, a putty knife, or a nylon pot scrubber. Clean the abrasive pad when it becomes clogged. Use paint thinner to clean oil-based strippers and water for water-based strippers.

3. Rub the cleaned surface with a fine abrasive pad and denatured alcohol to remove the last bits of paint and neutralize the surface. Rub with the grain of the wood. Let dry for at least 24 hours.

Wizard WARNING

Do not use cotton or terry-cloth towels with hot solvents such as lacquers, thinners, or solvents. Here's a true story about a friend who was refinishing furniture with an oil-based paint remover, working in his garage. At the end of the day, he hung his oil-soaked rags outside. Three days later he wadded up the now-dry rags and threw them in a plastic trash can in his garage. At 4 o'clock the next morning, my wife and I awoke to the sound of sirens. We looked out and saw that his garage and half his home were on fire. The rags ignited spontaneously. Use nonflammable shop rags. See page 150 for proper disposal methods.

Wizard WARNING

Lead and asbestos can be poisonous. Any home built before 1970 probably has materials in it that contain asbestos, and paint applied as recently as 1978 could contain lead. You may need to call a professional contractor to stabilize or remove these materials.

Lead

The older the paint, the more likely it contains lead. Years ago almost all paint included lead. With the development of latex paints, the use of lead content paints declined from the 1950s until lead limits were set for all paints in 1978. Dust and chips from damaged or degraded lead paint can contaminate your house and cause serious health problems for you and your family. For safety, any lead-bearing paint in your home that's loose, chipped, or breaking down should be professionally abated.

Asbestos

Asbestos has been linked to a number of serious lung diseases. Any home built before 1970 probably contains building materials made with asbestos—anything from sheet flooring to textured ceiling sprays. If these materials are in good condition, they are generally not a threat. The problem with asbestos occurs when the fibers are disturbed and released into the air.

You can cover an asbestos-containing surface, such as a textured ceiling, with new wallboard or skim-coat it with wallboard compound. Don't try to scrape the texture material off. If you want to remove it—or any material containing asbestos—hire an asbestos abatement contractor to take it off and dispose of it safely.

Test sticks, available at home centers and paint stores, reveal the presence of lead in paint. The tip turns red when rubbed over paint that contains lead. Follow the manufacturer's instructions.

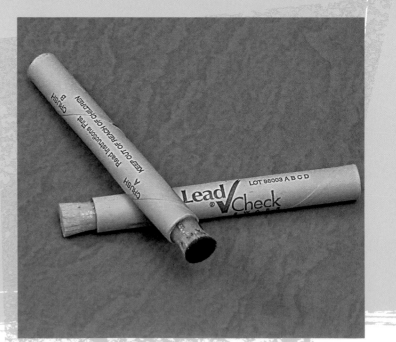

Working with a CONTRACTOR

Have you ever seen an advertisement for a carpenter with the slogan "We fix your husband's repairs"? They have a good point. Wall Wizards know when it is time to pocket the wand, clean out the cauldron, and call in a professional. Here are some tips to help you work with and choose a professional:

Always get written estimates that detail the job, no matter how small.

Never tell a contractor the price of other estimates you've received.

Expect a professional job, no matter the cost. If you want it done halfway, you could do it yourself.

Professionals should be on time. In this day of cell phones, there is absolutely no excuse for someone not showing up when they say they will or at least calling if they will be a few minutes late.

When an expected contractor arrives, ask to see a contractor's license and a driver's license. I can't tell you how many people have opened their doors and allowed me to walk right into their homes without asking for proof that I was who I said I was.

Never let a stranger into your home while you are alone. Call a neighbor or have a friend or adult family member home during the visit.

Ask to look at a portfolio of the contractor's work and ask for references with phone numbers.

Goodbye to WALLPAPER

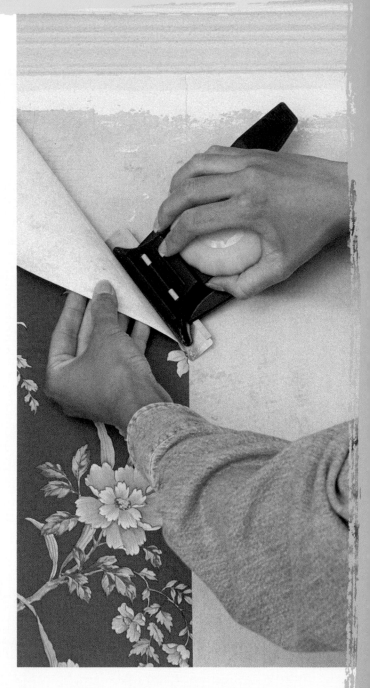

At every home show someone asks how to remove wallpaper. It's the No. 1 technique people want to learn. Even if you are only painting a room, chances are you will have to remove a wallcovering. Think of removing wallpaper as reverse hanging; the paper didn't go up in 4-inch pieces, so it shouldn't come down that way. The wallcovering should come down intact. Sound like magic? With a bit of wizardry, you, too, can remove wallpaper with ease.

The trick to removing an old wallcovering is to use tools and techniques that won't damage the surface or shred the wallcovering, while dissolving the adhesive that bonds the wallcovering to the wall. Wallcovering adhesives are based on simple starch binders. For easy removal, mix a special solution (page 65) that will attack the starch bonds between the wall and the covering.

The solution

In my Secret Stripping Solution, water is the vehicle that carries enzymes (the remover) that eat starch. Liquid fabric softener is a surfactant that makes the water wetter. When you add vinegar (a mild acid) and the baking soda (a base) together, they create a carbonic gas reaction that turbocharges the solution. Placing a plastic sheet over the wall forces saturated solution through the holes made by the Paper Tiger. The solution is trapped under a sealed, nonporous plastic sheet that prevents it from drying, so that the water-based solution can slowly break down the starch bonds that hold the wallcovering to the surface. TSP is an alkaline salt with a low pH. value that needs to be neutralized by a mild acid rinsing agent, such as white vinegar.

Other removal methods

The advantage of a gel remover is that it clings to the paper. It is especially effective for removing borders. Perforate the surface in the same manner as for wet removal, then apply the gel. Give it time to work properly in dissolving the wallcovering adhesive. Clean and rinse properly.

Steam removal is more dangerous than other methods, and it can damage the drywall behind the paper. If you do use a steam remover, perforate the surface in the same manner as for wet removal and then follow the manufacturer's instructions.

DRY REMOVAL

If the wallcovering is a fabric-backed vinyl or strippable solid-surface vinyl, you can probably remove its surface using a dry stripping method.

1. Begin by peeling the top edge of a sheet of wallcovering away from the wall, about 2 inches. Hold a dowel or broom handle against the wall and roll the paper around it.

2. Continue rolling the wallcovering around the dowel for about 8–10 inches. The dowel keeps the pressure spread evenly across the sheet of paper, which can help prevent tearing.

3. Hold the wrapped dowel firmly with both hands and pull straight down just above the surface of the wallcovering to minimize tearing the covering and the drywall's paper surface.

4. Because the nonporous vinyl surface has been removed, you can now easily remove the paper backing and old adhesive, using the methods on the following pages.

Wizard WARNING

Thinking about painting over wallpaper? Think again! Sure, you avoid the mess of removing the wallpaper, but the resulting finish is not as good. Wallpaper patterns and seam lines can show through the paint. Plus the paint can act as a solvent to the wallpaper paste, causing the paper to fall off the wall while you're painting, or bubble, wrinkle, and release irregularly over time.

There are a couple of instances where painting over wallcovering is acceptable. The first is when you need a quick fix—for a month or two—until you can actually do the job right. The second is when you paint over decorative wallboards, such as those used in modular homes. Since you can't strip the decorative coating off these wallboards the way you can with conventional wallpaper, painting over them is really your only option, and you can get surprisingly good results if the wallcovering is securely attached to the wall. Use a 150-grit sanding screen to smooth any irregularities and rough up the surface so the paint will stick. Dust the surface with a clean broom. Apply two thin coats of oil-based sealer, such as Kilz, to the wall. When it has dried, apply your finish coat.

WET REMOVAL

Use this method to remove more than one layer of wallpaper at a time.

1. Turn off power to the room and remove the electrical cover plates. Place a strip of waterproof duct tape over the exposed electrical plugs and switches to shield them from water. Cover the floors with plastic sheeting and an absorbent drop cloth, securing them along the edge of the moldings with duct tape.

2. Perforate the wallcovering with a Paper Tiger. Its rotary teeth penetrate the vinyl-coated surface, allowing the solution to soak through and soften the adhesive. Use two Paper Tigers, one in each hand, to save time. Start at the top left corner of a wall and work down and across the wall, making large circles. Poke about 10 holes per square inch; enough to score but not shred the wallcovering.

2

3. Next clean out a 5-gallon plastic bucket and brew up this secret solution.

Secret Stripping Solution
3 gallons hot water
22 ounces wallpaper
remover concentrate
¼ cup liquid fabric softener
1 cup white vinegar
2 tablespoons baking soda

4. Pour the mixture into a clean garden sprayer, pressurize it, and adjust the nozzle for a medium mist. Spray the walls from the bottom up, working around the room in one direction. Apply the solution at least three times around the room. Mix a fresh batch as needed. To ensure the chemical reaction is working effectively, move quickly; this solution remains active for only about 15 minutes.

5. When the walls are thoroughly saturated, smooth .7-mil plastic sheeting over the entire surface with a wallcovering brush and cut the plastic around the moldings to create a vacuum tight seal. The secret is to trap the solution under the plastic. Leave the plastic on at least three hours—overnight is better— allowing the solution to dissolve the adhesive.

6

6. To test whether the adhesive has released, pull back a lower corner of the plastic and with the paper scraper; gently scrape a seam open to determine if it is soft enough for removal. If the wallcovering resists, carefully lift the plastic about 6 inches away at the top of the wall and spray more solution to resoak the wallcovering. Then smooth the plastic back and let the solution work for an additional 6 to 12 hours.

7. When the adhesive has softened enough to remove the paper, fold about 4 feet of the plastic back toward a corner of the wall. Stick pushpins in the folded plastic so it doesn't fall down. Strip only one section at a time. Starting at the top of the wallcovering, lift the edge and begin scraping the wet paper backing off the wall. Position the scraping tool at a low attack angle to reduce surface gouging and damage. Spray on more removal solution to keep the paper moist; work from the top down, left to right. When that section is completely removed, fold back the next section of plastic and remove the wallcovering as described in the steps above.

7

Tips 'N' **TRICKS**

Any adhesive left on the wall can crackle the paint and prevent it from sticking successfully. To make sure you have removed all the adhesive, give the wall an iodine test. Mix 1 ounce of iodine with 1 quart of water. Use a trigger spray bottle to mist the wall. If the spray on the wall turns bluish purple, adhesive is still there and you need to continue cleaning. Test again and keep cleaning until you don't see any color. Spray the solution sparingly because iodine will stain if overused.

Clear Out and **CLEAN UP**

*C*leanup is just as important as any of the other steps you've already tackled. One point is worth repeating: An empty room is an easy room to paint. When everything has been removed, clean the floor and baseboards. Cover the floor with plastic sheeting, securing the edges to the floor with duct tape. Then add a layer of drop cloths to protect from splatters. Cover any remaining furnishings with .7-mil plastic sheeting.

CLEANING THE WALLS

Clean walls are essential for helping paint adhere. The wall should dry for a day before painting. This job is much easier when one person scrubs and another rinses.

First, dust off all surfaces with a vacuum cleaner or sweep with a clean dust mop. Set up two separate 5-gallon buckets with two sponge head mops, one for washing down the surfaces the other for rinsing off the dirt. Mark the handle of the mop used for washing with red duct tape to prevent mixing up mops when working. Fill your cleaning bucket with 3 gallons of warm water. For every gallon of water add ¼ cup TSP (trisodium phosphate). Mix well. Using a sponge mop with a scrubbing head, wash the wall in 8-foot widths, from the bottom up, working around the room. When you reach your starting point, turn the mop head around and begin scrubbing the wall with the nylon scrubbing head (wet sanding).

No matter what you're washing, change the cleaning solution often to keep from putting dirt and grease back on the surface. After wet sanding the first 8-foot section, use the rinsing solution immediately to remove the dirt and the cleaner off the surfaces. Fill your rinsing bucket with 3 gallons of warm water. For every 1 gallon of water add 1 cup of distilled white vinegar (a mild acid). Mix well. Using the rinse solution, wipe down with the second mop. Change this solution often. The vinegar acts as an astringent and neutralizes the phosphors that could prevent the paint from bonding properly to a surface.

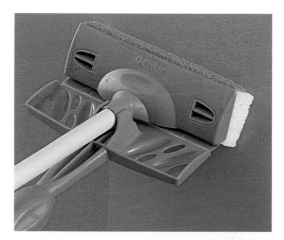

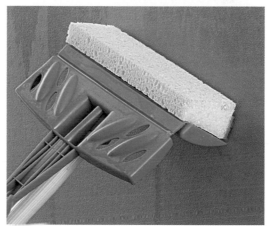

Tips 'N' **TRICKS**

Think your walls are grime-free? Try this test: Spray a tissue with water and lightly rub it on the wall. See that brown smudge? It's body oils, hair spray, and food oils that become airborne while cooking and eventually settle on the walls. Many paint jobs fail because new, clean paint is applied on top of dingy, dirty surfaces. Clean before you paint.

Tackling TOUGH STAINS

MILDEW

Regardless of where you live, you may be plagued with mold and mildew. Look for splotches on your walls. If you find some, dab them with a small amount of household bleach. If the spot comes off, it's not dirt—it is mold or mildew.

1. To remove mold and mildew, mix 1 cup household cleaner and 2 cups hydrogen peroxide in 1 gallon of warm water. Wear gloves and goggles. Apply the solution with a sponge or mop and let it stand for several minutes. Several applications may be needed. Rinse with a solution of 1 cup vinegar in 1 gallon of water.

2. When dry, lightly sand the places where the mildew appeared.

3. Seal against another outbreak by applying two coats of white-pigmented, oil-based sealer. Sand lightly between coats.

GREASE STAINS

Stubborn grease stains require an additional cleaning step. To remove, rub them with a liquid deglosser, such as Oops! or Goof Off, to break the oil film. When dry, sand with 120-grit sandpaper, then wipe away the sanding dust. Seal with two coats of white-pigmented, oil-based sealer. Sand lightly between coats.

RUST AND WATER STAINS

Rust and water stains will show through paint. To remove these spots, scrub with a solution of ¼ cup of Epsom salts in 1 cup of warm water. Rinse with a mixture of 1 cup vinegar in a gallon of warm water. Allow to dry for several days, then sand with 120-grit sandpaper. Seal with two coats of white-pigmented, oil-based sealer. Sand lightly between coats.

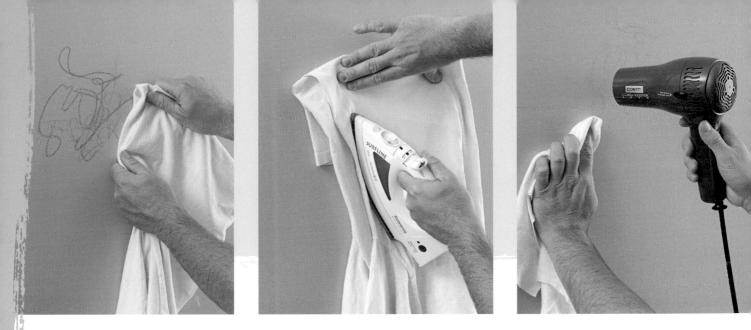

MARKER AND CRAYON STAINS

With three children, I've tackled more than my share of crayon marks on the wall. The best way to remove these stains is to fold an old T-shirt into a pad several layers thick and place it over a crayon mark, then set an iron at medium heat and run it over the pad. If it doesn't remove the crayon mark entirely, heat the mark with a hair dryer and blot away as much as possible. Seal with two coats of white-pigmented, oil-based sealer, sanding lightly between coats.

For scribbles from permanent markers, lightly dab the spot with nail polish remover. Rub the area with a liquid deglosser, such as Oops! or Goof Off. When dry, sand with 120-grit sandpaper, then wipe away the sanding dust. Seal with two coats of white-pigmented, oil-based sealer. Sand between coats.

Paint 10%

Application 10%

Prep work 80%

A successful painting job

Quiz the Wiz

Can't I just wipe the wall down and start painting?

I cannot stress enough how important it is to prep your walls before painting. Sure you can start painting without taking the time to follow through on prep work, but you're going to waste time and money because the paint won't flow, adhere, bond, or hide any of the imperfections on the wall. If you don't prep your walls, good luck—you're going to need it!

Cleaning CEILINGS

Ceiling work is awkward to do, but the results justify the work. The cleaning technique varies depending on the nature of the ceiling.

Smooth or lightly textured ceiling tile can be cleaned with a damp sponge mop. Smooth, previously painted ceilings can be cleaned this way: Mix 1 cup vinegar and 2 tablespoons baking soda in 1 gallon of water. Spray the solution on with a clean garden sprayer. Mop and rinse the same way as you would if cleaning a wall.

If the ceiling has a sprayed-on texture coating, first determine if it has been painted before. If it is unpainted, don't wash it; wetting the texture could damage it. Instead spray on an oil-based sealer to prepare the ceiling for a finish coat.

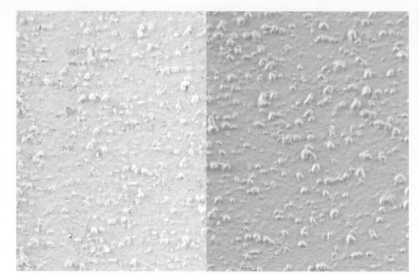

If a ceiling is unpainted (left), don't wash it. A painted surface (right) can be cleaned with a sponge mop and solution.

Cleaning BRICK AND CONCRETE SURFACES

Brick, concrete, and masonry require a different approach for cleaning. Scrub the surface with a nylon-bristle brush and TSP solution. Remove alkali deposits with a mixture of muriatic acid and water. Pour 1 cup muriatic acid into 3 quarts water. (Always add acid to water, never the other way around. Neutralize spilled acid with baking soda.) Scrub the surface with the solution and a brush. Rinse with water and let dry.

Coat the wall with a penetrating sealer as soon as possible after the acid solution dries. Masonry surface conditioner seals and hardens painted and unpainted masonry alike.

If the surface has flaking paint, scrub it off with TSP and a scrub brush, then rinse with a solution of 1 cup vinegar in 1 gallon of water.

Pressure washers can be useful for cleaning large areas of exterior masonry. However, you need to be careful that the water jet doesn't pit the surface or blast mortar out from between bricks, blocks, or tiles. Start low and gradually increase the pressure. If you begin to dislodge mortar or pit the surface, reduce pressure. If damage continues, go back to the TSP-and-brush method.

PRIMERS and SEALERS

Primers and sealers help ensure that paint or a wallcovering will adhere tightly to a surface. They provide a grip or tooth for materials on both porous and nonporous surfaces. They also provide color control for paint and make wallcoverings easier to strip.

Primer can be oil, shellac, or water-based. Primers are much richer in resin than ordinary paint, which gives them the ability to provide a better base for a final finish. By matching the primer to the finish color, you get all the benefits of priming and you don't have to apply a second coat of paint. Acrylic primers are synthetic materials suspended in water or plastic mediums and are usually cleaned with water. Shellac-based primers will adhere to nonporous surfaces and clean up with water and ammonia. Oil-derived primers can penetrate deep into porous surfaces and clean up with petroleum-based products.

Sealer, also called undercoater, is a prep coat that forms a nonporous layer when applied to a porous surface. It is also used to isolate problem spots like knots in wood and areas with mildew discoloration. Sealer products include oil-base undercoats, reactive resin, and catalytic epoxy. Most sealers have a white pigment (titanium dioxide) that blocks out dark stains and colors. Sealers can also block most common stains and control the growth of mold and mildew. Oil-based sealers usually clean up with hot solvents.

Use a sealer (left) before painting stripped wood (right).

Use a sealer (left) to prepare cinder block for painting.

Quiz the Wiz

How do I know when to use a sealer?

Use a sealer before painting porous surfaces such as these:

☆ Any unpainted surface, including new plaster, drywall, and old woodwork that has been stripped.

☆ Bare open-grained woods such as oak and maple.

☆ Bare woods, such as redwood, that bleed through or discolor paint.

☆ Large areas of wallboard joint compound or patching plaster.

☆ Masonry surfaces like unglazed brick, cinder block, and concrete.

☆ Metal surfaces; use an oil-based primer-sealer with rust inhibitors to prevent corrosion.

READY, SET... *One More Thing*

This last prep step will make painting faster and easier. All that is left to do is to cover exposed surfaces to protect from splatters and spills.

Think of masking systems as an inexpensive insurance policy that protects you from messy mistakes.

★ Dispense masking tape in as long a continuous strip as possible to prevent the paint from seeping between any gaps.

★ Firmly press the edge of the masking tape as close to the corner or line that separates one surface from another. Run a plastic tool quickly along the edge to set and seal the tape to the surface. For greater splatter protection, leave the tape sticking out.

★ Masking film is a powerful prevention system. Dispense and cut the film in one continuous strip from corner to corner. Set the tape firmly. Gently unfold the plastic and smooth it to the surface. The film clings to a surface so it won't flip up onto a freshly painted surface.

★ Wait for an hour after painting, then remove the tape and sheeting and dispose of it properly. It is biodegradable, so you can throw it away with your regular trash.

Painting from the PANTRY

How do you paint windows without getting paint on the glass?

Instead of spending hours masking off the glass, rub lip balm around the inside of each pane. When the paint dries, take a knife and score around the glass, then scrape the paint and wax away. If you still have wax on the glass, heat the glass with a hair dryer and buff clean.

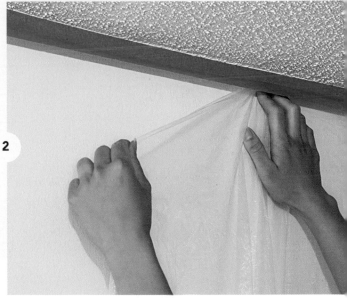

SEALING WALLS

If you are painting the ceiling or sanding a room, this essential step protects walls and woodwork from debris and drips.

1. Firmly press the top edge of blue masking tape along the top of the walls.

2. Slip the edge of the plastic sheeting under the open tape and press the tape down onto the plastic. The sheeting should drape down over the walls and baseboards. This technique can be also be used to create a barrier between adjacent rooms to contain dust and fumes to the work area.

Do not remove the sheeting until you are finished with the preparation, painting, and cleanup stages of your project.

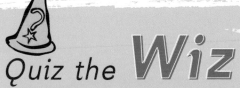

Quiz the Wiz

How can I keep paint from seeping underneath the edge of masking tape?

The secret to keeping this from happening is to heat-seal the tape. Run a tapered plastic tool quickly over the applied edge of the blue masking tape after you've set the tape. This heats the edge of the tape, the waxy adhesive on the tape melts, and when it resolidifies at the edge it creates a barrier that prevents paint from seeping underneath the tape.

chapter **3**

Painting *like a* Pro

Finally—it's time to paint! There's no mystery to painting a room; simply dip a brush into paint and apply it to a surface. That's why so many homeowners tackle painting projects themselves—because it seems like a doable home improvement project.

And so it can be, when you know the why behind the how-to. Applying paint is an easy skill to learn, but it takes planning, practice, and patience to become a Wall Wizard. Some techniques, such as mastering a paint roller, come fairly quickly. Others, such as holding a paintbrush correctly and using it to lay a flawless coat of paint on a surface, are more challenging—but still manageable.

Paint is a liquid that changes to a solid film. That may seem obvious, but it is the keystone of painting. The concepts and controls you'll learn in this chapter are the real secrets of managing paint. Paint as a material spreads easily and quickly, creating a durable finish. It can help cover imperfections, protect surfaces from wear, and resist discoloration and fading. And it's affordable. High-quality paint costs only about $24 a gallon, so you can transform a room for around a hundred dollars.

Besides prep work, the magic in a great job is knowing how to use the tools of the trade. This chapter focuses on choosing paint products and mastering a few basic application techniques that will help you produce professional-looking results.

MAKING THE GRADE
Learn all about paint grades, types, and finishes—page **84**

BASIC PAINTING 101
Handle the basic tools to achieve expert results—page **100**

WORKING A ROOM
Get the job done easier, faster, and better—page **108**

TOOLS That Rule

The right tools make a project go easier, faster, and safer. Here are a few basics for painting:

A **3-in-1 paint can opener** is the proper tool to use for opening a paint can. You can also use it to punch holes in the rim of the can so paint will run inside instead of outside the can and for resealing the lid without damage. Use a **tape measure** to determine the dimensions of a room so you will know how much paint you need. Two or three coats of **rubber cement** keep paint off door hinges and barrels.

The basic tool to deliver and manage paint as you apply it to a surface is a **2-quart plastic bucket**. This size bucket is also handy to mix a paint color and to use in cleaning up. Look for a brightly colored, plastic, square **paint bucket** with a built-in **paint grid**. It's a faster, neater way to evenly load your roller. It can hold 3–4 gallons of paint. I line mine with a heavy-duty plastic trash compactor bag and secure it to the rim with a small bungee cord. I can twist-tie off the top if I need to pause while painting, and when I'm finished painting, I just throw out the empty bag. You also can buy a separate grid to hang in your own bucket (get plastic rather than metal). Pro painters prefer a **5-gallon bucket** with a loading grid when applying paint to a room. It saves you from having to refill a roller tray; its size reduces the risk of spills.

If you're going to use a conventional roller tray, get a heavy-gauge metal one; it won't bend when you pick it up the way a plastic tray might. But what about rust and paint contamination? Never pour paint directly into a metal tray. Use a plastic disposable liner or a plastic bag as a liner. You'll save on cleanup time too.

Dishsoap bottles make great paint delivery containers. Clear plastic lets you see the paint color. They're easy to grip and squeeze to deliver the paint. The nozzle allows you to dispense the amount of paint you need, then seal the bottle airtight. A plastic **paint shield** protects a surface while you paint an adjoining wall or ceiling.

When painting, use a **box fan** to prevent fumes from building up. In a room without ventilation, put the fan in the doorway on the floor to blow fresh air into the bottom of the room, forcing contaminated air up and out the top of the doorway. For rooms with windows, put the fan in a window blowing outward. Open another window or a door (ideally as far from the fan as possible) to create a fresh air flow through the room.

Cool TOOL

Have a cleanup bucket ready at the start of any painting project. Why? Because the moment you open a paint can, you risk spilling it. Fill a 5-gallon bucket about two-thirds full of water and place a tile sponge in it. (You can use a smaller bucket for mobility.) Place this bucket in the middle of the room with a large towel beneath it. Use a damp sponge to absorb and clean up any spills; a rag will smear and spread the mess. Change the water often. Have plenty of shop rags or towels around to soak up water spills. Keep several other 5-gallon buckets with lids around for cleaning tools and mixing and storing paint.

PAINTBRUSHES

Paintbrushes are a Wizard's wand and are suited to painting woodwork, cabinets, and smooth-textured surfaces. An angled brush 3 to 4 inches wide is a good choice for most interior painting. Brushes work well for cutting in corners and edges because they spread paint efficiently and are easy to control. If you care for them properly, paintbrushes can last for years. Both of my brushes are more than 15 years old, and except for a paint fleck here or there, they look brand new. To choose your own brush:

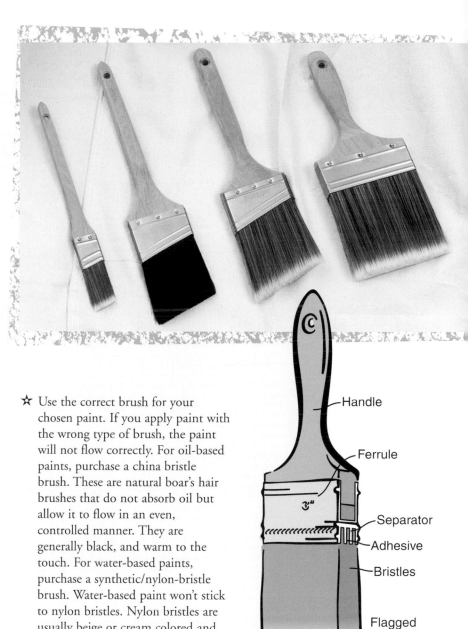

Handle
Ferrule
Separator
Adhesive
Bristles
Flagged ends

★ Look for one with a sturdy hardwood handle, a nonferrous or stainless-steel ferrule, and bristles tapered at their end so they form an even line when pressed against a flat surface.

★ Grip the brush by the handle; the handle should rest comfortably in your palm, fingers on one side of the ferrule, thumb on the other.

★ Fan out the bristles. Look for flagging: split ends on the bristles. More flagging in the bristles means a brush will lay the paint on the surface better.

★ Flex the bristles. They should feel springy, not limp or stiff.

★ Use the correct brush for your chosen paint. If you apply paint with the wrong type of brush, the paint will not flow correctly. For oil-based paints, purchase a china bristle brush. These are natural boar's hair brushes that do not absorb oil but allow it to flow in an even, controlled manner. They are generally black, and warm to the touch. For water-based paints, purchase a synthetic/nylon-bristle brush. Water-based paint won't stick to nylon bristles. Nylon bristles are usually beige or cream colored and cool to the touch.

Tips 'N' TRICKS

Take the "pain" out of painting. To avoid carpal tunnel syndrome, blisters, and cramps, make a soft grip for your paintbrush. Take 2-inch diameter pipe insulation, trim to the right length, and shove it over the handle of your paintbrush.

Quiz the **Wiz**

Can one brush work on a variety of surfaces?

Yes! A 3-inch angled sash brush is a good size for many painting chores. The angled bristles make it easy to see where you are painting. This brush works well for painting window sashes and cutting in edges.

Wizard **WARNING**

Have you ever walked into a hardware store and seen those bins overflowing with bargain paintbrushes? They are in the bargain bin for a reason. Besides giving you killer cramps in your hands, they absolutely will not lay paint evenly on a surface. They're good only for stripping—the black bristles are plastic, so they won't hold paint. They have no flag, which is essential for laying paint smoothly onto a surface. And the ferrule is made of tin, which rusts and can eventually contaminate the paint. Take it from the Wizard, even if you buy $100-a-gallon paint, if you use a 69-cent brush, you'll end up with a two-cent paint job.

ROLLERS AND PADS

Paint rollers

You'll be tempted to buy a cheap, throw-away fuzzy-napped roller, but save yourself the headache! A ½-inch **foam paint roller** works faster, easier, and better. You can load three or four times the amount of paint onto the roller. Such porosity means less dipping into the roller tray, which means more coverage in less time. Another advantage is that a foam pad will roll over any surface—texture, lap siding, stucco—because it is designed to conform to any surface it touches. A foam roller won't splatter paint or leave fuzzies in the paint on the wall. If you purchase a roller with a nylon core, it is easier to clean, and you can use it over and over. Yellow foam covers are designed for applying water-based paint. Gray or blue foam covers are used with oil-based paint.

When selecting a **roller frame,** choose heavy-duty plastic or stainless steel. Make sure the handle is comfortable to grip and has a threaded socket in the end so you can add an extension pole. Or buy a **frame with a telescoping handle.** My favorite has a handle that can expand from 12 to 32 inches, making it easy to roll the wall from floor to ceiling. A 4-foot **extension pole** works best; it's long enough to help you paint from floor to ceiling, yet short enough work in a closet. Get a fiberglass handle, not an aluminum one. Fiberglass will not conduct electricity, so if you should happen to make contact with a live outlet or fixture, you won't get hurt. Fiberglass also bends slightly, giving you better feedback on how much pressure you're putting on the roller.

Mini rollers are my new best friends. These 4-inch-wide rollers make it easy to paint small, tight surfaces, and they apply paint as evenly as the larger versions. Plus they paint into corners. Corner rollers, which are narrow and tapered to an edge, are ideal for getting into tight corners. The beveled shape and foam material is designed to evenly roll paint on both surfaces of an inside corner.

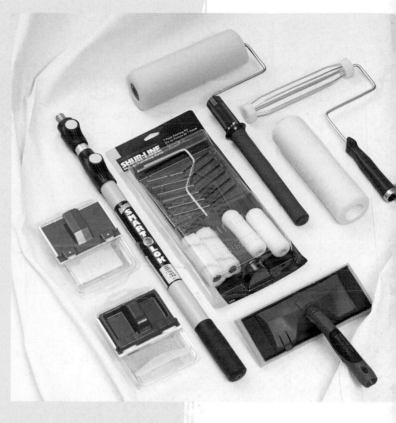

Paint pads

The 4-inch **paint pad** is a tool that has everything to offer: It's made of plastic, with a short, thick ergonomic handle. Tracking wheels set off the application pad from adjacent moldings. The bristle face of a pad is perfect for cutting in, edging, and painting flat trim. The pad's foam core holds three times more paint than a brush, has five times more surface area than a regular brush tip, and has bristles that are only ¼-inch long, so the paint won't dry out. It splatters and drips less than a brush. Most pads even come with a plastic paint tray and airtight snap-on lid.

Tips 'N' TRICKS

Slide a metal roller tray into a heavy-duty tall plastic kitchen bag, then press the bag into the tray to create a liner. If you need to stop, fold the liner over the tray to keep the paint from drying. To store paint in the tray overnight, seal it by dampening a large towel and draping it over the covered tray. The bag liner makes cleanup a cinch; simply turn the bag inside out and toss it in the trash.

Cool TOOLS

Nylon belt

Dusting brush and magnetic holder

Hook-and-loop tool hanger

Rag holder

5-in-1 tool and line

What good is a tool if it's not with you? That's the logic behind making a painter's tool belt.

☆ **Belt.** Begin with a 2-inch snap-buckle nylon web belt, available from home centers and hardware stores.

☆ **Rag holder.** Cut the top off a 1-liter plastic soda bottle at an angle to make a holder for rags or a package of baby wipes. Cut two slits in the back so it will slide onto the belt. This handy container prevents your clothing and skin from coming into contact with chemicals that seep from the rags.

☆ **Dusting brush and holder.** Cut the handle cut off a 4-inch polyester/ nylon paintbrush with a stainless steel ferrule. To hold the brush to the belt, use a 2-inch round pot magnet. Cover the magnet with duct tape to keep it from scratching the tool. Then fasten the magnet to the belt with a machine bolt, nylon locknut, and two fender washers.

☆ **5-in-1 tool and line.** Bolt a retractable lingerie clothesline to the belt and tie your 5-in-1 or other tool to the line. Attach another pot magnet next to the reel to hold the tool when it's not in use.

(Secure another pot magnet to the belt for holding other metal tools. The magnet is strong enough to hold a small hammer or screwdriver.)

☆ **Hook-and-loop hanger.** Apply the hook side of a piece of self-adhesive hook-and-loop tape to the belt. Attach the loop side to any other tools you want to keep on your belt.

☆ **Tool holder.** Make it the same as the rag holder for extra tools, such as a dish soap loading bottle, hand tools, or prep materials.

☆ If the belt seems too heavy to wear around your waist, add suspenders for support. If you want to, you can hang more tools on the suspenders.

Leave that ladder behind! You can work a room floor to ceiling and never have to climb a step—with make-'em-yourself bucket stilts.

I am vertically challenged, so I created bucket stilts to make it easy to reach the top of walls and trim. Buy two 5-gallon paint buckets with lids. Trace your shoe outline upon the lid and mark the attachment points at the toe and heel. Attach double-sided hook-and-loop straps to the lids with machine bolts, fender washers, and nylon locknuts. Secure the two shorter straps across the toes and the two longer straps at the heel to wrap around your ankles. Glue a large rubber pad to the bottom of each bucket to prevent slipping. Snap the lids onto each bucket, stand on the lids, and strap in. Now you are a full 18 inches taller than before and fully mobile. You can use store painting tools in the empty buckets when not in use.

SPRAY PAINT

If your job calls for a small amount of painting, or if you need even coverage on a small surface, spray painting is hard to beat.

Spray cans

Spray cans produce a fine, smooth surface if used carefully. A snap-on spray-can handle grip gives you better control when using a spray can. This inexpensive tool is designed to lock into the can top, providing a way of controlling the spray without holding the can. A trigger built into the grip depresses the spray nozzle on the can. The handle grip also protects the nozzle from being snapped-off inside the pressure valve, a common problem that renders the can and its contents useless.

Power sprayers

Sprayers are great for covering large surfaces, but they tend to use more paint than a brush or roller. They work well on irregular surfaces, such as louvered doors, panels, and wrought-iron trim. Inexpensive consumer models make sense if you have just a few items you need to spray and if you are patient. Follow carefully the directions for preparing and applying the paint and for cleaning.

The best spray tool for interior painting is a high-volume, low-pressure (HVLP) paint sprayer. It is more expensive than a typical consumer-model sprayer, but it produces less overspray and a finer finish than high-pressure sprayers. The HVLP sprayer can also handle almost any kind of paint and is much less finicky about viscosity, so it is less likely to clog. Preparations and masking are especially important when spray painting because everything that is not sealed or covered will end up with an overspray of paint.

A high-volume, low pressure (HVLP) paint sprayer is a great tool for interior painting. It spreads an even coat of paint on irregular surfaces, such as louvered doors or trim.

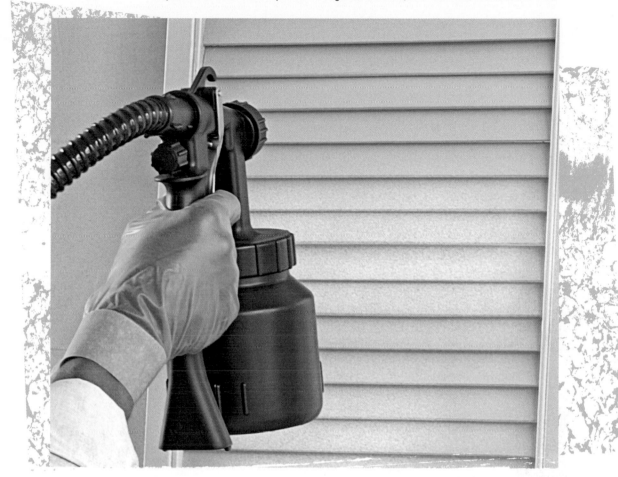

POWER ROLLERS

Here's some advice from someone who has tried all the gimmicks and gadgets on the market: If you're the type who jumps right into a project, don't invest in power rollers and sprayers. It takes practice to learn how to use them properly. By the time you've figured out how to put it together, fidgeted with viscosity flow, and fumbled your way through cleanup, you could have finished the paint job with a brush.

But once you become a Wizard of simple tools and techniques, you can transfer your knowledge to more industrial-strength tools, such as power sprayers, which can save you time and produce smooth finishes. Practice your technique on low-key projects before tackling high-visibility jobs. Try spraying shutters before kitchen cabinets or rolling the garage walls before painting your living room.

Making the GRADE

A Wall Wizard is frugal but never cheap—that's why you should always invest in the best tools you can afford. When it comes to paint, you get what you pay for, and if you pay for less, you'll get less coverage and lower quality results. It's easy to get confused in the store because there are so many different brands to choose from, each with a variety of additives and enhancers. But in reality, there are only three different grades of interior paint.

Low grade

The name says it all: low grade means low price means low coverage. It contains less durable binders, and it uses clays and other inert ingredients to provide coverage. This type is often referred to as professional-grade or architectural-grade paint. Low-grade paint is requested for commercial jobs— in offices or apartments—where frequent repainting is standard maintenance.

Medium grade

A medium-grade paint, also called decorator grade, contains a range of pigments and binders like those used in the premium grade. Medium grade is slightly less expensive than a premium grade.

This kind of paint is an effective substitute for high-grade paint when cost is a factor. Medium-grade paint can be a good choice when you expect to repaint every few years, such as when you redecorate children's rooms. It is also a good choice for low-traffic rooms like guest rooms or those where there is little wear and tear.

Low grade

Medium grade

High grade

High grade

When you buy the best, you won't be disappointed. High-grade paint is the most expensive type because of the added pigments and binders. It contains the most solid content of the three—up to 45 percent of the contents.

Yet that doesn't mean that your paint job will increase in price just because you use high-grade paint. Compared with a low-grade interior paint, a high-grade paint will spread more easily, splatter less, and show fewer brush marks. Also, because it contains more pigment, it hides flaws better. In the long run, a high-grade paint can actually reduce the cost of your project because it frequently requires the use of only one coat—a coat that, once dry, has a film that is 50 percent thicker than that of a low-cost paint. The result is a tougher, more durable finish that resists fading, yellowing, staining, and abrasion. These paints are more likely to be scrubbable too.

Many paints marketed at premium prices under designers' name offer special surface textures or effects that can enhance a room. Linen and other fabrics, stone, and other finishes are available in special colors. Some of these paints require special preparation or tools; all call for careful application in accordance with the manufacturer's instructions to achieve the full effect. Durability varies; ask your paint dealer whether the special paint you choose will stand up to your intended use.

Quiz the Wiz

Which paint is the best?

The best paint balances price and performance, and it should suit the project. You can use low-grade materials when it is applicable, such as for a rental property. On the other hand, high-grade paint is suitable if you don't want to paint as often. Your best bet is to thumb through consumer magazines that test materials on a nonbiased basis.

What's **YOUR TYPE?**

Paints today are manufactured with very high standards and quality controls that provide the homeowner with great color, performance, and cost-effectiveness. There are two types of paint: latex and oil-based.

Latex paint

My wife is the love of my life, but latex, or water-based paint, is a close second. It is versatile and easy to use; it dries quickly and cleans up with water (see page 129). It is nonflammable, almost odor-free, and resists fading, cracking, and chalking. A high-quality latex paint has 100 percent acrylic resin as its binder, while a low-quality latex paint has 100 percent vinyl resin. The latter decreases the durability of the paint. A top-quality latex paint has excellent adhesion to a variety of surfaces, including wood, masonry, aluminum siding, and vinyl siding.

Oil-based paint

Oil-based paint dries to a water-tight, impervious film. It goes on smoothly; its colors are deep and saturated. The film is extremely durable and has a greater resistance to fading in sunlight. On the down side, oil-based paints can sag during application, they take longer to dry and turn yellow with age. They can also seal moisture into wood that's not completely dry, causing it to rot. If surfaces are not properly prepared, oil-based paint can crack and discolor. Oil-based materials and solvents are bad for the environment: The fumes of their solvents degrade air quality, and both paints and solvents contaminate groundwater if not disposed of properly. Cleanup is more complicated than for latex paints (see page 130).

Latex paints offer many advantages over oil-based paints, including ease of application and cleanup, durability, versatility, and low impact on the environment.

Quiz the **Wiz**

How can I tell what kind of paint is on my walls?

Scrub a small out-of-sight area with detergent, rinse, and towel dry. Using a cotton ball soaked in ammonia, lightly rub the spot. If the paint comes off, it's latex. If not, it's oil-base.

THE ANATOMY OF PAINT

What can I say? Learning anatomy in biology class is definitely more exciting, but if you are apprenticing to become a true Wall Wizard, then you need to know the general makeup of a can of paint. Regardless of the type of paint, each kind consists of four basic ingredients:

Solvents are the liquid bases of paint: Water is the vehicle and the solvent for latex paints; petrochemicals are the vehicle and solvent for oil-based paints.

Binders are what hold the mixture together and make it adhere to a surface. They also give the surface a distinctive sheen, such as gloss.

Pigments are the finely ground powders made from minerals that give paint its color.

Additives are mixed in for a variety of purposes, from resisting mildew to enhancing durability.

Wizard WARNING

Reading the side of a paint can is about as much fun as reading IRS regulations. But you never know what you might discover in the small print on the label. Most labels include toll-free numbers for product-use information and emergency medical assistance. Words like "warning" and "caution" are exactly that—information about health and safety concerns that you should know. Here are some explanations to other commonly listed items:

☆ **Where to use.** Most paints list the surfaces on which they can be applied. Limitations also may be listed.

☆ **Coverage.** The standard estimate of 400 square feet per gallon is usually given, but some labels might indicate estimates for porous surfaces or how much to thin the paint for spray application.

☆ **Application.** Temperature limits, drying time, and time needed to dry between coats are listed here.

☆ **Information line.** You guessed it—this is usually the toll-free number to call for questions about paint or painting.

☆ **Paint care.** This is usually the manufacturer's recommendation on how long to wait before washing surfaces.

☆ **Contents.** What is inside? It should be listed here. Water tops the list for latex paint; alkyd is the first ingredient in oil-based paint. You'll find the common name along with a standard reference number that identifies the specific compound. For example,
CAS No. Ingredient
7732-18-5 Vinyl Acrylic
14808-60-7 Crystalline Silica

☆ **Limited warranty.** The information shown includes the length of coverage, conditions and exclusions, and how to make a claim.

STAINS

A stain colors the wood fibers while letting the grain show through. Stains may be a dye or a pigmented product with the consistency of thinned paint. Because the wood absorbs stain, it is important to add a clear finish coat for protection. Color-tinted clear finishes color and protect the wood, but they usually don't enhance the grain as much as a dye or pigment stain.

SANDING SEALER

No matter what kind of clear finish you choose, use the appropriate sanding sealer—water-based sealer for a water-based topcoat, oil-based sealer for an oil-based topcoat—over bare or stained wood before applying the topcoats. The sealer will make the topcoats lay more evenly, producing a finer finish and reducing the number of topcoats you need to apply.

SHELLAC, VARNISH, AND URETHANE

Unfinished oak

Oak with walnut stain

Paints disguise or camouflage a surface; topcoat finishes flaunt and protect whatever is underneath. Shellac is an age-old, all-natural finishing topcoat. It is made from the powder of ground up beetle shells suspended in an alcohol-based medium. This product is economical, nontoxic, fast drying, and makes wood look beautiful. It also seals out odors, which makes it an ideal finish for antique or second-hand furniture, which can smell musty with age.

Varnish works well for showing off the beautiful color and grain of display woods with a high-luster finish. Varnish is one of the oldest forms of clear-coat finishes and can be tinted to add a stain value. Both water-based and oil-based varnishes are available in sheens from satin to high gloss.

Polyurethane finishes are considered part of the varnish family. Most people prefer water-based varnishes because of their low odor and easy cleanup. Unlike paints, though, the oil formulations are still more durable than water-based clear finishes. High-resin polyurethanes are very durable, and spar urethanes, named for their early use on sailing ships, are the most durable of all, with outstanding resistance to weather exposure and ultraviolet rays.

Wizard WARNING

At long last, manufacturers have taken a look at paint through Wizard eyes and realized the importance of making paint more environmentally friendly. Lead, chromium, and mercury—all poisons—have been removed from almost all consumer paints, and chlorofluorocarbons (CFCs), which damage the ozone layer, have been eliminated from aerosol paints.

That leaves those nasty volatile organic compounds (VOCs) as the remaining environmental problem. VOCs are the petroleum-based solvents used to thin and clean up oil-based paints. They give oil-based paints a spreadable consistency and improve their ability to accept color. Likewise, small amounts of the solvent are also used in latex paints.

VOCs are a threat to the environment because their vapors escape into the atmosphere and become part of a complex chemical reaction that produces ozone, a component of smog. At the time the problem was identified, about 2 percent of the VOCs in the atmosphere came from paint. Many of these compounds are hazardous to people and require proper personal protection—hence my warning about wearing protective gear while painting.

Today, most latex paints contain no more than 10 percent solvent, and many contain only 4 percent to 7 percent. And solvent in oil-based paints has dropped from 50 percent to about 20 percent.

Painting from the PANTRY

I've been painting all my life and I still do not like the smell of paint! Here's a tip: To every quart of interior latex paint, add four drops of vanilla extract. You can also use other extracts, such as peppermint, as long as the alcohol in the ingredients is methyl alcohol, which is formulated to mix with water. Do not use perfume or other alcohol-based fragrances; they won't mix properly with water-based paint. Unfortunately there's no similar trick you can use with oil-based finishes.

BEHIND THE SHEENS

What happened to walking into a hardware store and buying a bucket of paint? Wall Wizards take the time to choose their paints carefully—after all, it is one of the key design elements in a room. One factor you must consider is sheen, the degree of light reflection off the painted surface. In other words, how much the paint shines.

Sheen affects the finish's appearance, durability, and suitability for certain uses. As the amount of sheen increases, so does the enamel value, which determines the hardness or protective value of the coating. Manufacturers use many names to describe the different paint sheens, such as eggshell. Because sheens are not standardized, one manufacturer's satin or semigloss paint can be shinier, or glossier, than that of another. Here are the most common finishes:

Flat

Flat paint has the least amount of shine because it has a nonreflective, matte finish that hides surface imperfections. It is a good choice for concealing bumps or dents and patched cracks and nail holes. It has been used traditionally for surfaces that get little wear and tear because it absorbs grease easily and does not stand up well to frequent scrubbing. New products, however, do have some built-in scrubability.

Flat paint works well on older interior walls and ceilings that have been repeatedly painted and repaired and for rooms that were once wallpapered because removal sometimes leaves visible scrape marks.

Gloss

Semigloss

Satin

Flat

Satin

Satin paint, more recently known as eggshell, has a soft luster similar to the sheen on the shell of a fresh egg. It is more durable and stain resistant than flat paint and suitable for woodwork where a slight sheen is desired. Satin paint is easier to clean than flat paint and does not highlight surface imperfections like a gloss paint. Use a satin luster for children's rooms, hallways, and baths.

Semigloss

Semigloss paint has a higher sheen than satin paint and is even more stain resistant and easier to clean. However, the light-reflective quality of a semigloss luster can highlight surface imperfections. Semigloss paint is a good choice for surfaces that are subject to wear and frequent scrubbing: kitchens, bathrooms, halls, and children's rooms, as well as woodwork and cabinets.

Gloss

Gloss paint is the most durable, stain-resistant, and easiest to clean of all paints. With its hard, shiny surface, it's also tougher and virtually hides brush strokes. Glossy colors are intense, a characteristic that can highlight surface imperfections and overpower a room. This type of paint is excellent for areas exposed to heavy traffic, like kitchen and bathroom walls, and all woodwork, including banisters, railings, and cabinets.

Quiz the Wiz

How can I choose the best sheen for a room?

Here's a handy chart to decipher the sheen of paint.

Area	Paint	Why
Ceiling	Flat	Uniform nonreflecting appearance hides flaws
Living room, halls, bedrooms, children's rooms	Satin	Resists stains and has a lustrous appearance
Bathrooms and kitchens	Satin or semigloss	Stain resistant; easier to clean than flat paint
Kitchen cabinets, woodwork windows, bathrooms, kitchens	Gloss	Durable and easy to wash

HOW MUCH PAINT *do you need?*

Too much or just the right amount? That's the question when trying to figure out how much paint to purchase. It is handy to have a little extra paint on hand for touch-ups, but who wants to spend the money and be stuck with more paint than you need?

If you're not a numbers person, the following steps may sound like gibberish. Just take it slowly and break out each step—at the end you'll arrive at an accurate estimate for the amount of paint you need.

1. Calculate the square footage of the surfaces to be painted. Measure the length and width of the room and determine its perimeter, which is the distance all around the room. For example, if the room is 13 feet wide and 18 feet long, its perimeter is 62 feet (13 feet + 13 feet + 18 feet + 18 feet).

2. Multiply the perimeter by the room's height to get the square footage of wall space. If the room is 8 feet high, then its square footage is 496 square feet (62 feet × 8 feet).

3. Count the doors and windows in the room. Subtract from your wall area 21 square feet for each standard door and 15 square feet for each standard window. (If your room has large doors, such as a sliding patio door, or large windows, you can measure the width and height of each door and window, then figure the exact square footage of each. You don't need to be precise; round to the nearest square foot.) The room in the example has one standard door and three standard windows, so subtract 66 square feet (21 square feet + 3 × 15 square feet) from the wall area. The answer is the amount of wall area to be painted: 430 square feet (496 square feet – 66 square feet).

4. To find the number of gallons of paint needed, divide the wall area by 300—the square footage easily covered by a gallon of interior paint. In the example, you would need a little more than 1.4 gallons to paint the walls; round that up to 1½ gallons—one gallon and two quarts.

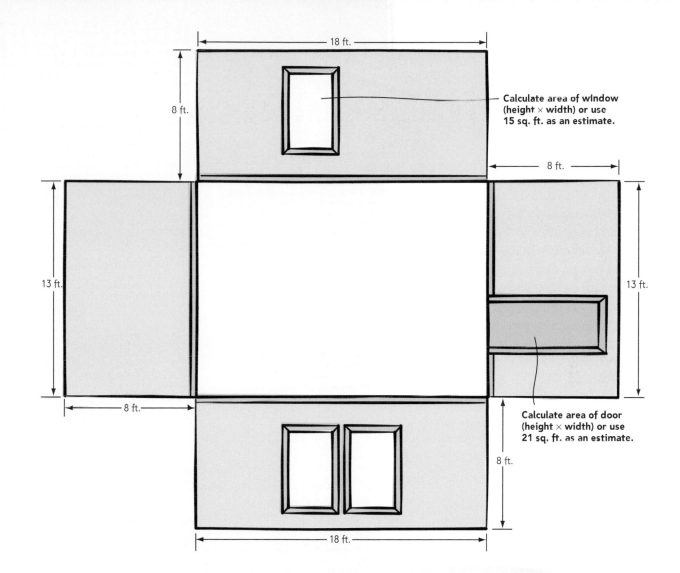

18 ft.

8 ft.

Calculate area of window (height × width) or use 15 sq. ft. as an estimate.

8 ft.

13 ft.

13 ft.

8 ft.

Calculate area of door (height × width) or use 21 sq. ft. as an estimate.

18 ft.

8 ft.

Tips 'N' TRICKS

After that lesson in estimating, you'll be relieved to learn these tried-and-true Wall Wizard tricks.

☆ A gallon of paint will cover about 300 square feet of wall area. Some manufacturers stretch it to 400 square feet, but go with the lesser amount to keep from running out of paint in the middle of a job.

☆ Always buy more paint than you need. This extra amount allows for spillage, waste, and spots that soak up more paint than expected. Plaster, for example, is more absorbent than wallboard. Also, you'll want leftover paint for future touch-ups. Remember to buy extra paint if you plan to paint the interiors of built-in bookshelves or cabinets.

☆ Another reason to buy more paint? Custom-mixed colors vary slightly from batch to batch, so it's best to buy enough paint at one time instead of running out and having to match the colors.

☆ If you can't decide between 4 or 5 gallons, go with 5 and buy it in a 5-gallon container. It should actually be cheaper than three 1-gallon cans, and you're guaranteed the colors will be the same.

SHAKE IT UP, *Baby!*

It's time to go shopping! If you're organized, purchase everything you need for painting at one time, from tools to drop cloths to paint. Likewise purchase all the paint you need at one time so that the colors are a match from one can to the next.

If you know this project is going to spread out over a few weeks, however, wait to buy the paint until you're ready to brush it on the walls. This way, it will be freshly mixed, and you won't have to take it back to the store for mixing or try to mix it yourself. If you buy a pre-mixed color, don't forget to ask the dealer to shake the can on a mixing machine.

If your paint has been sitting longer than a week, take it back to the dealer and have them reshake it on the mixing machine, or mix it yourself using a propeller-type attachment on a drill.

Tips 'N' TRICKS

Mixing paint yourself can be messy. Here's how to prevent paint spattering as you mix it with a power drill and attachment. Poke the mixer shaft through a paper plate, then hold the plate against the open top of the can while mixing.

Prepping *PAINT*

Another step that separates wannabes from Wizards is taking the time to box, strain, and condition paint.

BOXING

If you have several cans to use for a job, the color can vary from can to can. Ensure a uniform color by mixing all the paint together, a technique known as "boxing."

Pour all the paint into a clean plastic 5-gallon bucket. Mix it until it is uniform in color. Pour the boxed paint back into the cans. Tightly seal the lids on all but the can you're ready to use.

STRAINING

Straining eliminates lumps in the paint. If the paint has separated, stir the thick paint up from the bottom of each can to free as many lumps as possible. Then box the paint, pouring it all together through a nylon paint strainer and into the bucket.

Paint less than one year old usually doesn't require straining. Older paint might have a thick skin on the top; remove the skin and set it aside. Box the paint, pouring it through a nylon paint strainer into the bucket. When the skin has dried, wrap it in newspaper and discard.

CONDITIONING

Paint stored for a year or longer may need conditioner to improve its flow, adhesion, and coverage. New paint can be conditioned too. The conditioner adds elasticity and retards drying, making it easier to maintain a wet edge during painting—important for reducing overlap marks. I use paint conditioner on almost every job I do.

Following manufacturer's instructions, add a conditioner such as Floetrol to water-based paint; add Penetrol to oil-based paint. Most paint that is more than three years old should be tossed out (see page 135)— unless, of course, you stored it using the Wall Wizard technique (see page 132)!

The Three
LAWS OF PAINTING

It's time to lay down the law—the three immutable laws of painting. These are the secrets of painting. Use them to control the paint in its liquid state. Understanding and utilizing these laws dictates the way you apply paint. To be a Wall Wizard, you have to master the medium, so it does not master you.

Law 1 – *Never paint out of a paint can.*

☆ *Container contamination.* As you paint, your brush picks up dust, grease, grime, fly boogers, spider snots, and other spots. When you dip into the can to reload, all that debris ends up back in the can, contaminating the paint. That causes flecks and specks in the paint finish.

☆ *Dangerous drying.* If you ever have painted from an open, full can, you probably noticed as you worked that the paint became gooier, stickier, and thicker. This is the air reacting with the exposed paint, which is setting up in the can, not on the wall.

☆ *Material mover.* A paint can is strictly a storage and delivery container. It was never designed to be painted from or carried around; it's too awkward and heavy. You are more likely to knock it over and spill, especially the gallon size.

Law 2 – *Pour no more than ½ inch of paint into the container.*

☆ *Material management.* Pour only ½ inch of paint into a plastic bucket to stage and control it before application. This forces you to refresh the paint more often, keeping it in its liquid state for better flow and bond to the surface.

☆ *Lighter load.* With only ½ inch of paint in your bucket, you carry less weight, work faster with better control, and avoid fatigue by the end of the job.

☆ *Spill spoiler.* Because you have only ½ inch of paint in the bucket, if you happen to stumble, the paint is less likely to spill out. And if you do happen to spill, there's less to clean up.

Law 3 – *The enemy of paint is air.*

☆ *Air wars.* The air around us is the drying agent for paint. Paint doesn't dry in a sealed paint can, but the minute you open the can, air rushes in and starts the drying process. Limiting paint's exposure to air until the paint is where you want it to be is a way of controlling the project.

☆ *O_2 factor.* In simple terms, oxygen is the reactor that turns paint from a liquid to a solid. Exposure to air thickens the paint, creating drag during the application, producing brushstrokes in the finish.

☆ *Cap it.* Reduce paint's exposure to air by immediately replacing the lid on the paint can. Cover your working container (bucket or tray) To seal a can for storage, use the techniques described on page 132.

Wizard WARNING

It goes without saying that Wall Wizards take proper safety precautions. Always take every step possible to protect yourself from potential disasters. Here are some reminders:

☆ Shut off the power at the circuit breaker for the room you are painting or wallpapering.

☆ Follow the manufacturer's instructions and safety precautions for all products.

☆ Keep paint products out of the reach of children.

☆ Protect your eyes by wearing safety glasses or goggles when working overhead, using strong chemicals that may splash, or creating or cleaning up dust. Wearing a full-face shield is also a good idea when working overhead or with solvents.

☆ Turn off all sources of flame, including pilot lights, when spraying any solvent-based compound or paint.

☆ Secure all scaffold planks. Extend the plank 1 foot beyond a support at each end and clamp or nail it into place. Do not step on the plank between its support and its end.

☆ Create a proper, secure storage area where you can keep materials and tools, especially sharp ones, when not in use.

★ **Check the manufacturer's label on your ladder to make sure that it can support your weight plus the weight of the tools or materials you will carry up it.**

★ **Keep pets and children away from work areas.**

★ **Use a scaffold on stairs. Place an extension plank on the stairway step and a step of the ladder; make sure it is level.**

☆ Step down and move the ladder instead of stretching.

☆ Position an extension ladder so the distance between its feet and the wall it leans against is one-fourth of the ladder's height. Most extension ladders have a sticker on the side showing the proper leaning angle.

☆ Follow the manufacturer's instructions when you operate power painting equipment.

★ **Create a flow of fresh air through the room to prevent fumes from building up. Put a box fan in the doorway or window.**

☆ Don't work with solvent-based chemicals if you are pregnant or have heart or lung problems.

☆ Rinse oil- or solvent-soaked rags and spread them out to dry—don't wad them up. Dispose of them carefully. If you want to reuse rags, launder them thoroughly and spread them out to air-dry.

☆ Open the legs of a stepladder fully, lock the leg braces, and make sure the ladder sits level and steady on the floor.

☆ Never stand on the top step of a stepladder, its braces, or work shelf.

☆ Never let small children near open containers. Always cover a 5-gallon bucket with a snap-down lid.

Basic Painting 101

Because the paint finish is only as good as the surface to which it's applied, start your project by cleaning, repairing, and preparing all the surfaces in the room. Here are the practical methods and techniques for applying finish coats on the most common interior surfaces.

Break your work down into logical steps and procedures. Don't rush; set plenty of time aside for each task. Think safety; most accidents result from lack of awareness and overestimating your abilities.

In general, work down and out of the room; start with the ceiling, then walls, then floors. This concept will provide you a consistent starting and ending point. The best wall to start on is the door wall, so your skills are honed by the time you reach the more visible surfaces across from the entrance.

Complete tasks, don't skip around from project to project, stay focused, and follow the procedures and techniques for the best results. Drying takes time; don't rush the paint, allowing enough time between coats for best results. And finally, RELAX! Enjoy the process; the results will be worth your time and effort. It will give you a sense of accomplishment, satisfaction, and success.

Tips 'N' TRICKS

Here's a great control concept: Line your paint pot with a large resealable bag. Open the mouth of the bag and pull down over the edge of the bucket rim. Secure with a large rubber band. Now, if you need to pause from painting the bag can be closed to prevent drying. If you need to change colors, drop in a new bag. Cleanup is a snap—just throw the used bag away.

OPENING ACT
Your opening moment has arrived—pry open a can of paint.

1. Use a 3-in-1 or 5-in-1 tool to gently open the paint can. Do not use a screwdriver; it will bend and distort the lid shape.

2. Dab a spot of the paint on the side of the can and the can lid. This quickly identifies the type of paint sheen and color inside the can.

3. Slide the wet paint lid into a plastic zip-closure bag or the plastic pouches left over from making a trash-bag apron (see page 33). Sliding the lid into plastic prevents the paint from drying, stops the lid from dripping paint, and provides a clean lifting tab to be able to open, pour and close the can as needed.

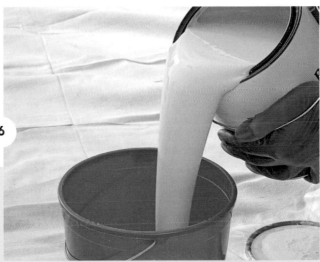

4. Punch holes in the groove inside the rim, called the lid well, with a hammer and nail or with the sharp point of the 5-in-1 tool and a mallet. The holes allow excess paint to drain back into the can. This technique will also ensure that after the project is finished, the lid can set and seal properly into the can for storage.

5. Lightly stir the paint.

6. Pour only ½ inch of paint into the paint bucket.

7. Be sure to place the lid back on the paint can; remember—the enemy of paint is air.

Cool TOOL

Make a power paint pot. Take a 2-quart plastic bucket; make a small hole in the side about 2 inches down from the rim. Fasten a 3-inch pot magnet on the inside with a machine bolt, a nylon locknut, and two fender washers. Put duct tape over the magnet. The magnet will hold the brush by its metal ferrule to keep it from sitting on the bottom of the bucket, which would overload the brush and bend the bristles. Add a flexible handle made from duct tape. Put a short piece, sticky-sides-together, in the middle of a longer piece. Attach the tape to one side of the bucket, around your hand, and up the other side. Remember the tool rule: Make the tool hold you, so you don't have to hold the tool.

BRUSH WORKS

HANDLING A BRUSH

A paintbrush is a paint detail tool. Its design is based on way you use it. It seems simple, but people spend thousands of dollars learning how to hold a golf club, so it's only fitting that you learn the proper way to hold and use a paintbrush.

★ Always hold and use your painting tool in your dominant hand. As you work, keep the tool in front of your face; you will have better physical and visual control.

★ Hold the brush firmly with your thumb on one side of the ferrule and your fingers spread across the opposite side. You can also grip the brush like a pen or pencil, letting the handle rest comfortably in the hollow where your thumb joins your hand.

★ Use long sweeping strokes to apply and spread out the paint. These broader movements will give you better leverage and minimize muscle fatigue.

Typical grip
Grip the brush lightly, with your thumb underneath and your fingers on top of the ferrule. Let the handle rest in the joint where your thumb joins your hand.

Trim touch
Hold a small trim brush like a pen or pencil, with the handle resting in the hollow of your thumb joint.

Wizard WARNING

Take care of yourself! Painting is one of the most repetitive, stressful jobs you can do with your hands. I have carpal tunnel syndrome from all the years I have spent painting. To help avoid the same fate, pay careful attention to what I tell you on this page about how to properly hold and use your tools. *You* are your most important tool—use it with care.

DIP, WIGGLE, PAT: LOADING A BRUSH

A paintbrush is designed to lay paint on a surface, not to store it. Here's how to control the tool and the paint.

Dip your brush into the paint. Since you have only a ½ inch of paint in your paint pot, you can't overload the brush bristles or force excess paint into the ferrule. **Wiggle** to load paint into the bristle tips of the brush. **Pat** both sides of the brush lightly against the inside of the pail as you lift it out. This will release any excess paint from the bristles so they don't drip. Never scrape your brush on the side of the bucket—you'll break bristles and damage the tool.

Three strokes—you're on!

Gravity is your friend, so work from the bottom of the wall up with strokes about 16 to 24 inches long. Apply the paint in three strokes for a smooth finish:

1. The first stroke is always up to unload the brush.
2. The second stroke is gently down to set the paint onto the surface.
3. The third stroke is up to smooth the paint and remove brush marks.

Apply the paint quickly, moving up and along the wall, painting from bottom to top, moving forward between strokes. While moving at the end of last stroke, lift the brush tip off the surface to "feather" the paint back into your wet paint. This step will help the paint blend evenly onto the surface. After you have laid on a section of paint, make one continuous, final stroke to eliminate the overlapping sections and bristle stroke marks. Don't brush over the freshly painted surface until it has thoroughly set, or you will gum up the finish.

1

2

3

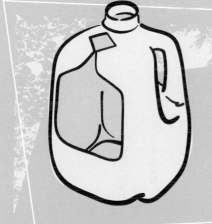

Cool TOOL

A recycled plastic milk jug makes managing paint during a project easy. Cut an opening as illustrated. Stop about 2 inches from the bottom. Cut an inverted V-shaped slit and a diamond-shaped hole near the neck of the jug to hold your brush. To hold it easily, slip your hand into the handle with your palm toward the jug. When finished, pour unused paint back into the can using the jug top as a funnel. Stretch an old nylon stocking over the opening to filter the paint. You can clean and reuse the jug or toss it in the trash.

PAD WORKS

HANDLING A PAINT PAD

A pad is the ideal detail paint tool. A little understanding and practice will help you use this high-tech tool to lay paint faster, better, and more evenly on any surface.

☆ Look for complete paint pad kits. The plastic packaging for the kits is also the loading paint tray and an airtight lid.

☆ Make the tool hold you: Make a flexible handle. Place the empty tray in your hand, palm side up, then stick a piece of tape down one side of the tray, loosely over the back of your hand, and up the other side.

☆ Always hold and use your painting tool in your dominant hand. Grip the pad handle firmly as you paint. Keep the tool in front of your face; you will have a better view of your work and better physical control of the tool.

☆ The tracking wheels—that's what got you interested in this gizmo in the first place, right? You thought they would eliminate having to use masking tape. Wrong. Even though pads are designed to deliver the paint right up to the edge of adjacent surfaces, they are not foolproof. What can easily happen is that when you load the pad, paint gets smeared onto the wheels and they leave little paint marks along the wall or ceiling or trim. Take out some painting insurance—masking tape!

☆ Load the pad and tray often. This prevents the pad from drying out.

☆ Use long sweeping strokes to apply and spread out the paint. These broader movements will give you better leverage and minimize muscle fatigue.

☆ If you need to stop painting for a short time, set and store the pad inside the tray and snap on the lid to stop the paint from drying in the tray.

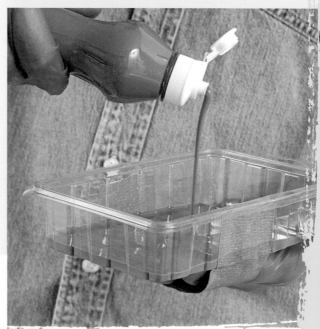

DIP, WIGGLE, SCRAPE

A paint pad is designed to evenly load and lay paint to a surface. Don't overwork this tool. Here are some techniques that will give much better control.

1. Dip the pad into the paint. Pour only ¼ inch of paint into the loading tray. This amount won't let you overload the pad bristles, or let the pad sink into the paint, or easily spill the tray.

2. Wiggle the pad to load the paint into its bristles and foam core. This action will pump in, load up, and lock in the paint.

3. Scrape the pad gently across the edge of the tray. Don't press too hard; you want the bristles to be full of paint, but not dripping. The excess paint will flow back into the paint tray. This lets you control the load amount going onto the surface.

DIFFERENT STROKES

Remember that gravity is your friend, so work from bottom to top and from side to side with strokes about 24 to 36 inches long. You'll need only two strokes for a smooth finish.

1. Place the loaded pad firmly on the surface. The first stroke is always in one direction to unload the paint in the pad.

2. The second stroke runs gently back over the area in the opposite direction to set the paint and remove bristle marks. At the end of this stroke, lift the pad while moving to feather back into the wet paint. This will help the paint blend evenly onto the surface.

Apply the paint quickly, moving up and along the wall, painting from bottom to top, moving forward between strokes.

Cool TOOL

Make a micro paint grid. Cut a rectangle of #14 stainless steel screen mesh slightly larger than the inside dimensions of the paint tray. Measure in ¼ inch from the screen edge and bend the screen down to form the legs of the grid. Place the grid inside the paint tray. It prevents the pad from sinking too deep into the paint and getting paint up into the tracking wheels.

ROLLER WORKS

A sponge roller and roller frame are the perfect tools for painting large surfaces. Screw in an extension pole on the end of the frame for better leverage as you work. Here's the best way to hold, control, and use this simple painting system:

DIP, RAKE, AND ROLL

Get the tool ready to paint to improve the coverage and quality of your paint job.

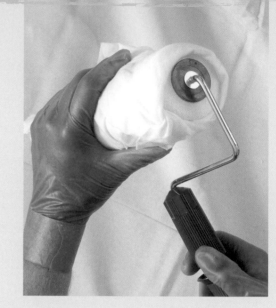

1. Start by slightly moistening the roller cover with water (if you'll be using latex paint) or paint thinner (if using oil-based paint). After dampening the cover, wrap a clean shop rag around it and blot dry.

2. Pour ½ inch of paint into your paint tray (a plastic-lined metal tray) or a bag-lined bucket and loading grid, if you have a lot of painting to do. Fill a paint bucket no more than one-third full).

3. Using quick but firm strokes, roll the roller down the slope of the tray, called the rake, and gently dip into the paint well to load the tool. Try not to slosh the roller around.

4. Slightly lift the roller directly above the tray and move it back up to the top of the rake. Roll the roller slowly down the slope of the tray. Repeat this procedure several times to load the cover properly. Try not to spin the roller as you do this; it will splatter the paint. Work the paint deep into the roller. Keep rolling down the rake until the roller is evenly coated with paint but not dripping.

Cool TOOL

Have you ever accidentally spilled, stepped-in, or knocked over the paint tray? Then you'll love this Wizard tool: Make a paint bucket trolley! Buy a large, round plastic planter base with casters. Get a 5-gallon bucket and a length of 2-inch foam pipe insulation. Cut the bucket off about 10 inches from the bottom. Center the bucket on the plant dolly and attach with screws. Apply the pipe insulation around the rim of the plant mover to make a bumper. Set a painting bucket with loading grid into the cut-off bucket and you're rollin'.

LET'S ROLL

A paint roller is designed to roll paint on a surface, it is not meant to splatter it. Do not overload this tool and do not roll quickly. With your paint roller loaded and conditioned, approach the wall.

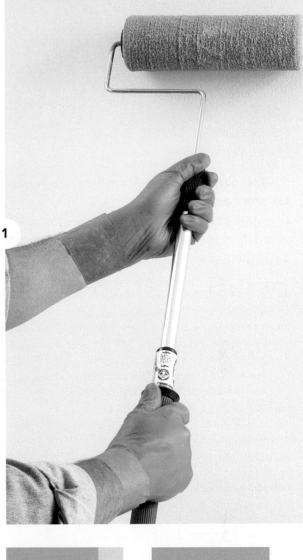

1. Hold the roller frame and pole firmly with the both hands. Place your dominant hand at the bottom end of the pole for more control. Place your other hand in the middle to act as a leverage point that will mechanically triple the amount of force applied to the roller. As you work keep the tool in line with your body; you will have better balance, stamina, and vision.

2. Position the roller so that the open end points the direction you are painting. This keeps the roller from sliding off the roller frame.

3. Apply the three-stroke rule:
☆ The first stroke is always up to unload the paint roller. Don't roll too fast. Doing so will cause the roller to splatter paint. Use long, continuous strokes to apply and spread the paint. These broader movements will give you better leverage and reduce muscle fatigue.
☆ The second stroke is down to set the paint onto the surface.
☆ The third stroke is up to smooth out or lay-off the paint finish. As you begin your third stroke up, twist the roller extension pole slightly in the direction you are working. This move puts more pressure on the leading end of the roller—the one that hits the unpainted part of the wall first—to deliver maximum paint where it's needed. It also creates less pressure on the trailing end of the roller, the end on the wet side of the paint job. This helps eliminate the ridges of wet paint (snail trails) that are caused by too much roller pressure.

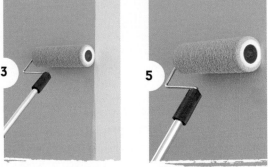

4. Work from the bottom of the wall up. Moving across the wall and working in sections—about three or four roller widths wide and the full height of the wall—continue loading the roller with paint, using the same stroke techniques across the entire length of the surface. Reload the roller cover often. Keep the roller cover moist and saturated with paint. A thoroughly loaded roller cover will make the paint flow more easily, to cover the surface better.

5. After you have painted about 8 feet of wall, lay off the paint by lightly rolling an unloaded roller from the top of the wall to the bottom. This keeps the surface sheen looking consistent and eliminates the "V" effect when the paint dries.

6. Keep moving forward. As with any application tool, keep a wet edge of paint.

Working a ROOM

It takes two ... two people to effectively paint a room: the cutter person and the roller person.

Choose the right person for the right job. Break down your plan into logical and manageable steps. Identify, define, and divide the workload into separate but equally important tasks. One person uses a brush or a pad to apply a narrow band of paint around the room where one surface meets another. This is called cutting-in. The other uses a roller and extension pole to continuously and consistently apply the paint to the large surfaces. This is called rolling-out.

If you're detail oriented, handle the cutting-in and trim work. If you're stronger, paint with the roller. Working in a team of two makes the job twice as fast and half as tedious, saving you energy, time, and money.

Stay focused on your assigned task, because the more you do something, the better and faster you become. Your satisfaction level will rise, and your results will look even better.

Direction connection

If you're right-handed, you will find it easier to paint from left to right. If you're left-handed, work from right to left. Begin painting from the corner behind a door or closet. The cutter paints out from a corner, then the roller comes behind and rolls the paint over the wet cut-in band. Continue working around the room this way.

Of course, one person can paint a room working alone, but it takes much longer, and it's harder to keep the paint flowing and maintain a wet edge. If you must work alone, paint in small, manageable sections and work quickly but methodically.

Wizard WARNING

Don't cut-in an entire room and then roll-out the walls. What happened to maintaining a wet edge? It dried, of course, creating visible overlaps. When you apply the wet roller over the dried cut-in band, the paint creates an overlap called "hat-banding." To correct this problem you will have to apply two to four coats of paint, which will require more paint, time, and effort.

Hit the WALLS

CLEVER CUT-IN

Be sure to mask all surfaces that you don't want to get paint on. Cut-in first, applying the paint swaths about 4 feet ahead of the roller person. Firmly grip the loaded tool with your dominant hand and apply the paint, keeping the tool in front of you. Have a platform ladder handy so you can easily reach all the surfaces.

Working in one direction, lay a 3- to 4-inch-wide band of wet paint along the inside edge of the wall. The wet band creates a dividing line of paint from one surface to the other, a "safety zone" so the roller person doesn't roll too close and get paint on the adjacent surfaces. Work from the bottom up, applying around the edges, first along the baseboards about 4 feet, then up and along the inside corners, and finally across at the ceiling line.

After you have laid on about 5 to 6 feet of paint, make one continuous, final stroke to eliminate overlap and stroke marks. Do not continue stroking the painted surface; doing so will gum-up the finish.

Clean small application tools, such as pads and brushes, about every two hours (see pages 129, 130).

Quiz the Wiz

Should I paint the wall first or the trim?

Great question! If you are an amateur painter, do the trim work first (see page 112-113), then the walls. This strategy will make it easier to sand, prepare, and paint all the details, edges, and planes of the trim work. After all the coats of paint on the trim work are thoroughly dry, mask off the trim work and paint the wall. Because you have masked the trim, any splatters from the wall will land on the masking tape, which will be removed later. Most professional painters would paint the wall first, then skillfully do the trim.

ROOM ROLL-OUT

The roll-out should be applied only after the cut-in has been done and the paint is still wet. Be sure to tape down drop cloths to protect the floor and give you safe and sound footing. Attach an extension pole to the roller frame or use a telescoping handle. Load the roller cover with paint. Position the loading tray or bucket just ahead of your work section to keep you moving forward and reduce your body movements. It also helps prevent roller dripping and bucket spills. Properly load the paint roller and start at the section to be painted. Keep the tool saturated with paint. If you must stop for a time, close up or wrap the tray and roller to keep them from drying.

Body position and mechanics are an important part of fast and effective painting. Stand with your feet spread about shoulder-width apart, always with your body facing the direction you're going to paint. This position, called the "A" stance, gives you better balance and leverage to reach bottom to top in one continuous stroke.

With the roller loaded, position yourself in front the section you want to paint. Place the roller on the surface and apply the paint to the wall. To avoid paint splatter, don't roll fast, but work at a comfortable rhythm and pace. After you have applied and laid-off two or three roller widths on the wall, take a step forward and repeat the same procedures. The cutter and the roller should be spaced no more than 4 to 6 feet apart; this spacing ensures the roller is always painting into the wet edge. Continue working around the room in this manner until it is completed.

Tips 'N' TRICKS

Pull the masking tape while the paint is fresh! Remove the masking materials within 45 to 60 minutes after the paint is applied and set to prevent surface tear up. The idea of masking tape is to protect surfaces from the paint, however when you slop the wet paint over the sealed masking tape, then let the paint cure to hard, the paint film is now bonding to both the wall and the masking tape. In the past, as you removed the masking tape, the film acts as one piece, and will tear and rip up the wall or trim work. It's definitely easier to remask an area then to repair it!

CEILING *Solutions*

Ceilings pose a special challenge to even the most experienced Wall Wizard because you are working upside down. Before you start painting, cover the floor and any remaining furniture or appliances in the room.

Use a 4- to 6-foot telescopic extension pole on your roller frame. This keeps your feet firmly on the ground. It also makes the job go easier and faster because you don't have to move and climb up and down a stepladder. And because you're farther from the roller, you're less likely to get splattered. If you're going to paint a room's ceiling, do so before painting any other surface in the room.

First, remove the light fixture and ceiling fans and mask the appropriate surfaces. Clean and prepare the surface properly. Begin by cutting in about 4 feet starting from the corner farthest from the room's entry door. It's all right to slightly overlap down onto the wall. This will save you time as you paint the ceiling and walls. Because you will be cutting in around each wall, the wall paint will cover this overlap. Alternate between cutting-in and rolling-out, working in sections across the ceiling and using the three-stroke method—out, in, out. The last stroke should always be in the same direction as the first to keep the sheen consistent.

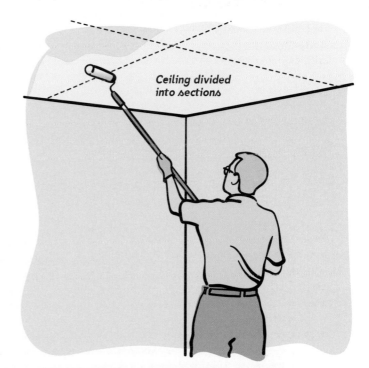

Ceiling divided into sections

Quiz the Wiz

Does it matter what the weather is like when I paint?

Yes, weather can make a difference when you are painting. Paint flows and bonds best when the humidity and temperatures are moderate. For most of the country, that means the best time to paint is in late spring or early fall. In hot, dry environment paint dries too quickly, before it has a chance to level out, leaving a poor finish quality. In a humid environment, paint takes forever to dry and can sag and droop. If you have to paint in less-than-ideal conditions, use paint conditioner as described on page 95. In addition use a humidifier to add some moisture to the air in dry conditions, and a dehumidifier to extract some of the moisture from the air in humid conditions.

TRIM WORKS

The architectural embellishments such as crown moldings, doors, baseboards, and window casings are called trim. They are usually constructed of wood, vinyl, or metal. If finished well, these surfaces are what people most admire about a project.

Because trim such as door or window frames can be exposed to weathering, thoroughly repair and prepare the surfaces to ensure the paint's bond and finish. Trim work is easy to paint; it just takes a steady hand and the patience to work slowly and methodically. Be certain to mask all wall surfaces.

Work from the moldings at the top of the wall down to the baseboards to avoid drips on the finish coat you just applied. Use the three-stroke rule for application.

Always paint with the grain and length of the trim work. Paint horizontal sections with horizontal strokes and vertical sections with vertical strokes. Treat each trim piece as a separate section. Apply the paint quickly. Work each separate trim piece from the bottom up, keeping a wet edge. At the end of last stroke, lift the brush tip off of the surface to feather the paint back into the wet paint. This will help the paint blend evenly onto the surface. After you have finished a section of paint, make one continuous, final stroke to eliminate the overlapping sections and bristle marks.

Tips 'N' TRICKS

To make your final finish magical, apply two thin coats of paint rather than one heavy coat. Allow the first coat to dry thoroughly, then lightly sand the surface with a 240-grit sandpaper in the direction you are laying on the paint. Clean the surface. Apply the second coat for the finished effect. The first thin coat dries faster and bonds better to the surface. The second coat deepens the color coverage. With one heavy coat, you run the risk of the paint sagging, creating a poor finish quality.

WINDOW WORK

Casement and sash windows are a big part of trim work. Windows can be tricky to paint, but when you break the job down into steps and stages, it's easier to do. Because windows are exposed to weather, thoroughly prepare them for painting. Repair any mechanical problems to ensure their proper operation.

Remove and store all the hardware so you can clean, prepare, and paint the surfaces without damaging it. Mask the appropriate surfaces. (Remember the lip balm trick? See page 72.)

Paint the windows at the beginning of the day, so they will be thoroughly dry by the time you want to close them. Use a combination of rolling and brushing for a beautiful finish. Apply the paint with a 4-inch closed end foam roller, then stroke the finish out with the paintbrush. This technique allows the roller to deliver the paint quickly and evenly onto the surface, while the brush lays off the finish. Begin applying the paint to the deepest part of the window, working to the shallowest part, and from the farthest outside corner in so you're never reaching over wet paint. Work in the same direction as the grain.

Apply two coats of paint for the best results. When the finish is thoroughly dry, replace all the hardware.

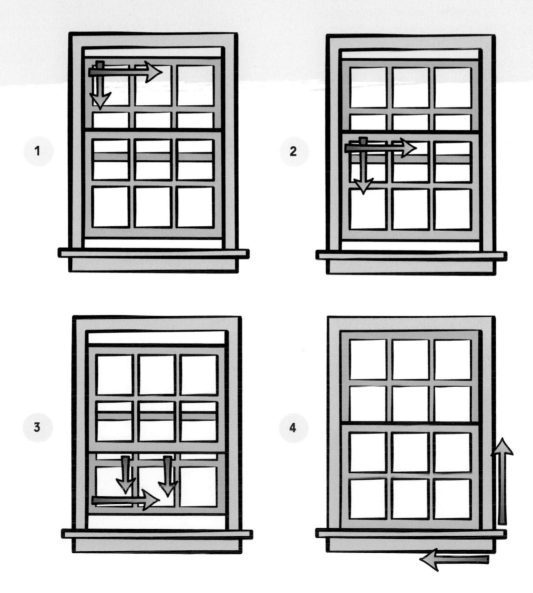

Painting DOORS

DOOR DETAILS

Doors, frames, and casework are all considered trim work. They are usually constructed of wood, vinyl, or metal. Because doors are the entrance and exit points, plan to paint them last, so the paint finishes will be undisturbed and allowed to dry upon completion of the room. The easiest way to paint a door is while it is in its frame, on its hinges. Clean the hinges with rubbing alcohol, then mask them with two coats of rubber cement (peel the cement off when finished). Prep the same as window trim. Remove or mask the doorknobs, lock, and other hardware.

For any type of door, start by painting the frame (casing), working up from the inside bottom, across the header, and down the striker side.

To paint a **flat door,** start by painting the inside hinge edge, working around the door in one direction. Use a combination of rolling and brushing, applying the paint with a 4-inch closed-end foam roller (1). Run two or three roller widths the full height and across the door face, then lay off the finish by brushing from bottom to top with a lightly loaded brush (2). This technique allows the roller to deliver the paint quickly and evenly to the surface while keeping a wet edge and leaves a smooth brush finish.

1

2

HOW TO PAINT A PANELED DOOR

Your approach is a bit different to paint a **paneled door**. Apply the paint with same roller and brush techniques. Begin by painting each panel, starting with the upper left-hand panel (1) working down the door face in sequence (2, 3, 4). Starting from the bottom of each of the center vertical stiles (5, 6) lay down and brush out the paint. Next, working from the top member (7) down, continue painting each horizontal member (8, 9). Finally, paint the full-height outer stiles (10, 11) and edge (12). Lay-off any runs or sags as you paint.

Allow the paint to dry, lightly sand, and apply the second coat. When the paint is dry, score around the edge of the hinges with a knife and peel away the cement. Replace the hardware.

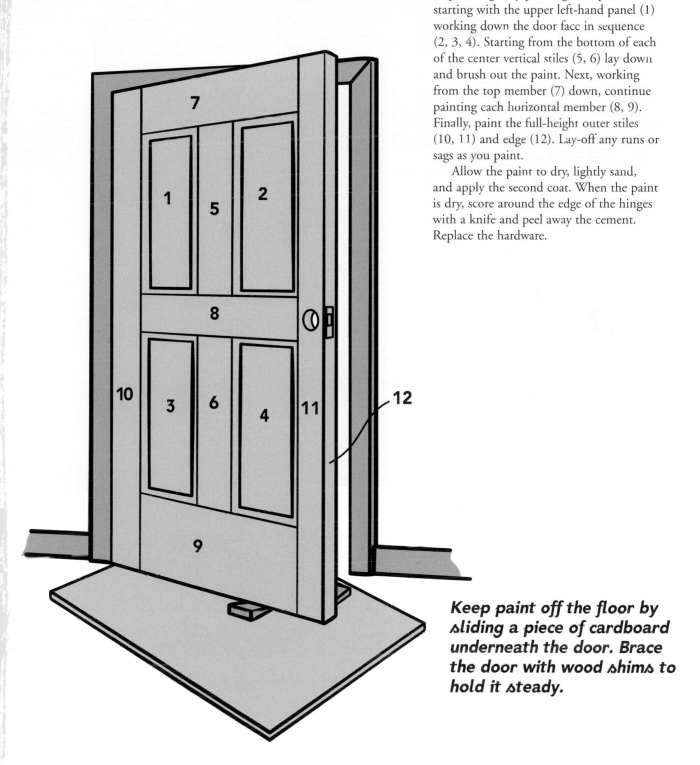

Keep paint off the floor by sliding a piece of cardboard underneath the door. Brace the door with wood shims to hold it steady.

Painting with a *POWER SPRAYER*

Can't resist the temptation to use a power sprayer? To ensure your success, take time to learn the Wizard's way of operating and painting with one.

Today's high-volume, low-pressure (HVLP) paint sprayers drastically reduce overspray, which was one of the major drawbacks of spray painting inside a house. These sprayers are relatively easy to adjust and operate, and they apply a smooth, even coat. They produce a fine finish on small surfaces, such as furniture or cabinetry. Items that would be difficult or tedious to paint neatly with a brush or roller, such as louvered doors or heat grates, are easy to paint with a sprayer. A sprayer is also ideal for painting textured acoustical ceilings; some manufacturers offer a right-angle nozzle especially for ceilings.

The general steps for spray painting follow:

1. **Thin the paint.** The consistency is specified by the manufacturer to ensure a smooth spray finish. The sprayer comes with a viscosity cup or similar testing device to gauge the paint consistency— fill the cup with paint and watch how long it takes to flow out through a hole in the bottom. Pour paint into a bucket and thin it with the appropriate thinner to deliver the correct viscosity.

2. **Strain the paint.** Do this as you pour it into the sprayer's paint cup. Straining prevents clogging and uneven painting.

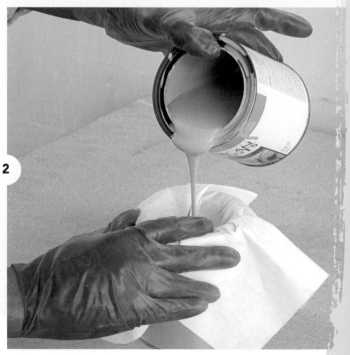

3. Adjust the spray gun. Follow the manufacturer's instructions; spray the paint onto a test piece of plywood or cardboard when making adjustments.

4. Practice, practice, practice. If this is your first time using a sprayer, practice on a piece of plywood or cardboard first. Point the nozzle toward the surface and begin spraying from side to side in a 20-inch-long pass. Keep the gun the same distance from the surface as you spray and don't swing the gun in an arc. Pull the trigger upon moving the gun and stop spraying before you stop moving the gun. This prevents paint buildup and sags at the ends of the passes. Move the gun at a steady speed—the actual speed depends on the distance from the surface and the size of the spray pattern.

5. Build the color in several thin coats rather than applying one heavy coat. Overlap the passes to avoid streaks, runs, and sags.

SPRAY PAINTING FROM A CAN

A snap-on handle will give you better control and make the job easier. Be certain to shake the can well. Use in a well-ventilated area. Move the can parallel to the surface you're painting. Spray two thin coats; the first from the bottom up, the second from left to right, allowing each to dry. This creates even coverage, and the paint dries faster. Depress the nozzle after you start moving the can and release it before you stop. When finished, turn the can upside down and spray out paint to clear the nozzle.

Tips 'N' TRICKS

Here are a few more tricks I've learned in my years as a Wall Wizard.

★ If bristles come off the brush, remove them from the painted surface with eyebrow tweezers or by touching them with the wet brush—they should cling to it. Wipe the brush with a clean cloth to remove stray bristles.

★ Wipe paint off a paint shield after each use to keep the edge clean.

★ Disposable foam brushes don't work well for paint; they tend to drag it across the surface rather than let it flow. They do work well for varnishes, stains, and shellacs, creating glass-smooth finishes with few brush marks.

★ When painting with enamel, work quickly and brush lightly. Overbrushing leaves streaks and marks. Do not touch up areas you've already painted. If you have problems, let the paint dry, degloss it, and repaint.

★ Use a sprayer to paint heating system registers and grills.

★ For quick touch-ups: Pour a small amount of paint into a clean shoe polish bottle; the pad is perfect for small jobs. Label the bottle with the room and color; snap on the lid to store.

★ Before you start painting, fill a couple of 1- or 3-gallon buckets with clean water. Have a synthetic tile sponge and plenty of towels handy throughout the job. Use them to quickly wipe up any spills. Change the water often; don't put dirt back up on the surface. Dry the surface with a clean, dry towel to prevent water spots and stains.

★ A concave roller does a great job on fixed shutters, radiator fins, and other rounded surfaces.

★ You can make your own brush for small touch-ups. Simply clip a clothespin to a piece of sponge foam. Cut the point any shape you want to paint into corners or hard-to-reach places.

★ A beveled paint roller helps prevent paint buildup in corners.

★ Paint pipes, wrought-iron balustrades, and other contoured surfaces with a paint mitt.

Painting *PANELING*

Yes, you can paint paneling, but why? If you have real tongue-and-groove or beaded-board paneling, it's worth keeping and refinishing. Otherwise, remove it or cover it with drywall. But if none of those solutions are practical, you can paint it if you prepare the surface.

1. Make sure the paneling is secure to the wall studs. If you find any gaps or bowing, use wallboard screws or ring-shank paneling nails to level and stabilize the panels. Locate the studs behind the paneling; drive the fasteners into the studs just beneath the surface of the paneling.

2. Clean the surfaces and rinse to degrease and degloss the surface. Allow the paneling to dry overnight and apply a coat of white-pigmented oil-based sealer. Let it dry. Lightly sand the surface with 180-grit sandpaper and dust off the surface. Apply a second coat of sealer and let it dry.

3. Fill the grooves and any holes with exterior grade surfacing compound. This material bonds and flexes better with the wood as it expands and contracts, preventing gaps and cracks that can emerge in time with regular wallboard joint compound. When the compound is dry, sand smooth and wipe clean. Apply a second coat of exterior grade compound; two or three light coats are better than one heavy coat. Finally, apply the third coat of sealer, let dry, and sand smooth.

4. Now you can safely install wallpaper, faux finish, or paint the walls because you have stabilized, sealed, and smoothed the paneling.

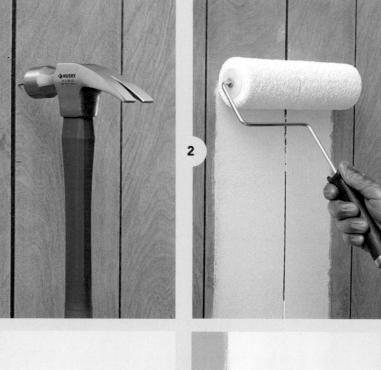

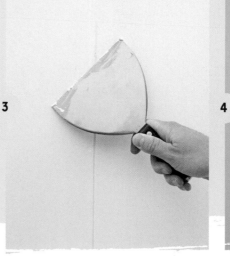

Painting COUNTERTOPS

LAMINATE COUNTERTOPS AND MELAMINE

Although you might be tempted, don't paint kitchen countertops. Ordinary paint isn't a food-safe finish, and it won't stand up to the heat, moisture, and abrasions that kitchen countertops are subjected to daily. On the other hand, if you have a little-used guest bathroom with a dated surface, you can update it quickly and easily with paint, and light use shouldn't damage the finish if you do it properly.

Begin by sanding the surface with fine-grade sandpaper to lightly scuff away the gloss, not sand away the color. Wipe clean. Next, lightly roll on a coat of primer for nonporous surfaces, such as Kilz. When it is dry, roll on a base coat of latex paint. Use a roller to avoid brush strokes in your finish.

When the latex paint is dry, apply three to five coats of clear-drying latex polyurethane, making sure each coat dries before adding the next one. You can use spar varnish for even greater durability, if you don't mind the yellowing effect this coating will have on the paint underneath.

For melamine shelving and cabinets, lightly sand the surface, but take care not to damage the melamine surface. Wash with a TSP solution. When dry, roll on a thin coat of primer for nonporous surfaces, such as Kilz. Finish by rolling on two coats of latex paint.

Don't attempt to paint over scratched or water-damaged melamine—those surfaces should be replaced.

Painting *BRICKS* and **CONCRETE**

Bricks, concrete, and other masonry surfaces call for some extra prep steps because of alkali and their coarsely textured, porous surface.

One problem is efflorescence, a white, powdery deposit that occurs when water migrates through concrete and mortar, then evaporates, leaving a mineral residue. Wait at least six months for concrete or mortar to cure before painting. Before painting dry masonry or concrete, repair active leaks and remove the alkali deposits (see pages 50–51).

Seal the surface with a masonry sealer, then apply a coat of paint using a foam roller cover. Keep the sheen consistent and smooth by rolling in one direction only. Latex masonry paint works well on most interior masonry surfaces, including brick.

PAINTING CONCRETE AND BRICK FLOORS

Make sure the surface is dry, moisture-free, and patched, if needed. Clean the floor with TSP according to instructions.

If you plan to use oil-based paint, etch the concrete with a solution of one part muriatic acid added to 10 parts water. For latex paint, use a phosphoric acid solution in the same ratio. Both acids are caustic chemicals, so exercise caution. Mix the solutions in a plastic pail, adding the acid to the water. Never pour water into acid; it can boil and splash out. Wear rubber gloves and safety goggles while mixing and applying, and follow manufacturer's instructions.

When the floor is dry, vacuum up any dust, apply a sealer, then roll or brush on the finish coat (see page 124 for floor paints).

For high-traffic areas and concrete exteriors such as garage floors, use epoxy paint. It dries harder, lasts longer, and is impervious to oil and stains. One caution: epoxy paints are slick. You might want to add special silicate, available from a home supply store, to create a nonslip surface. Many specialty masonry paints are available for surfaces such as floors and stairs. Ask a paint retailer to help you select the best kind of masonry paint for your surfaces and conditions.

Painting FLOORS

Tired of that old linoleum or wood floor? Paint your floors! It seems like a gutsy move, but trust me, it's one of the easiest and most inexpensive ways to freshen a room. Wood floors are perfect choices for painting. Vinyl sheet linoleum and tile that is in good condition can also be painted, but remember that the embossed pattern will show through and that the paint job might not last very long.

CHOOSING PAINT

Paint floors with standard interior paint and enamel. You can also purchase specialty floor paint. Which one is best for your job?

☆ **Oil-based paint** creates a hard film and covers a surface better than latex. Moderate color selection.

☆ **Latex paint** gives a more flexible film. Best suited for extremely low traffic areas and surfaces. Wide color selection.

☆ **Alkyd or modified epoxy latex** porch and floor paint is great for high traffic and wet areas. Color selection is limited.

☆ **Industrial enamel** is the toughest kind of oil-based paint available. The high gloss makes the surface slippery, but you can add nonslip grit to the paint. Very limited color choices (about five).

☆ **Porcelain epoxy paint** is the most durable and expensive coating of all because of the chemical makeup. Professional installation only. Custom colors and sheens.

PAINTING WOOD FLOORS

You know what I'm going to say—you've got to prep the surface before painting. After cleaning and prepping, seal problem areas with an appropriate sealer, prime with an appropriate primer (your paint dealer can help you with your selection of undercoatings), and roll or brush on the finish coat, working from the farthest corner to the doorway.

PAINTING VINYL FLOORING

Ordinarily, I don't recommend painting vinyl and linoleum flooring. The surfaces don't accept paint well and are likely to be dirty, stained, or waxed, which further inhibits paint bonding. And painting won't hide holes or dents. If at all possible, tear up old flooring and replace it. But if you absolutely have to have a quick fix for a single event, for instance, and aren't worried about long-term durability, you can dramatically change a room's look.

Before painting vinyl that's in sound condition, test the paint on an inconspicuous spot to make sure it will look OK when complete. Sand the vinyl with 220-grit sandpaper to dull the shine. Wipe clean and then apply a liquid deglosser to improve bonding. When dry, prime the floor, then roll or brush on one or two finish coats.

chapter **4**

Clean *and* Store

CLEAN AS YOU GO
Cleanup is what you do
throughout your job—page **128**

STORAGE SOLUTIONS
Protect your investment in tools
and materials—page **132**

THE DISH ON DISPOSAL
Proper handling protects you
and the environment—page **135**

Admit it—you'd rather toss your tools
than go through the rigmarole of proper
cleanup, storage, and disposal. It's not that
you're lazy; it's just that when a project is
complete, you want all the stuff to go away,
right? Ignoring a problem isn't going to
solve it. If you maintain your tools and
work area continually, your painting
experience and results will be much better.
In this chapter, you complete the painting
cycle by understanding the why behind the
how-tos of cleaning, washout, storage
and disposal.

By the way, would you like to learn
how to clean a brush in 10 seconds or less,
without throwing it away? Read on.

CLEAN as You Go

Cleanup is not the last thing you do; it's what you do throughout your paint project. For starters, it's easier to wipe up wet paint than it is to chisel dry paint off a surface. Here are some more helpful tips:

✫ Maintain your workspace. Centralize the tools in one area. Place them on your project table so you can find them throughout the job.

✫ Wipe down, sweep, and vacuum frequently so debris will not settle into the surface finish.

✫ Cleanup any paint splatters or spills immediately. It is easier to absorb up wet paint than it is to chisel off hardened paint.

✫ Set up a large, lined trash can in a convenient location. Constantly pick up and throw away used masking tape, plastic wraps, and other debris as you work. Having a messy workspace prolongs the job and makes it more dangerous.

Clean works!

Teamwork applies to the final phase of your painting project.

Divide to conquer. Identify, define, and divide the various tasks into logical and manageable steps. Working in a team of two makes the job twice as fast and half as tedious, saving you energy, time, and money.

Stay focused. Stick to your assigned role and task. Clean from the ceiling down, working down and out of the room.

Be thorough. Observe and repeat procedures to ensure quality control.

Reassemble the room

Once the work is finished and the paint has dried, remove all the coverings and clean the room again. Remount all the switch plates, towel bars, drapery hardware, vents, and grills. Turn the power back on at the circuit breaker panel. And finally, take a moment to admire your handy work and enjoy the beautiful colors and finishes. But not too long; you've got more cleanup to do.

Cool TOOL

Just because a brush and roller spinner is so much fun to play with doesn't mean it's not a practical tool. In fact, this tool cuts drying time for brushes and paint rollers to about one minute. Simply push your brush or paint roller into the spinner, pump the handle, and voila! The water is eliminated from the bristles or roller.

1

Total TOOL CARE

Taking care of brushes, rollers, and pads will save you time, energy, and money. Don't throw your tools in a bucket or sink and expect them to clean themselves; they'll be ruined, and you'll end up throwing them away and buying new ones. A Wall Wizard knows: It's no pain to maintain. Clean your brushes every two hours while working with water-based paint and at the end of your project.

WASH OUT WATER-BASED MATERIALS

Here's how you can clean water-based paint from brushes and paint pads in 10 seconds:

2

1. Remove excess paint from the brush or pad by scraping it with the edge of a 5-in-1 tool or the teeth of a brush-cleaning tool.

2. Mix up several gallons of this magic potion in a 5-gallon bucket: For every gallon of warm water, add ½ cup of fabric softener. The fabric softener is a surfactant—it actually makes the water wetter, so it can more easily dissolve paint.

3

3. Dip your brush into the mixture, swish briskly through the water, and count to 10. The paint will release from the bristles and settle to the bottom of the bucket.

4. To dry your paintbrush quickly, use a paintbrush spinner to fling water from the brush. Spin the brush in a wet waste bucket. To make one, start with an empty 5-gallon plastic bucket with lid. Cut an 8-inch hole in the center of the lid. Place a plastic trash bag in the bucket and snap on the lid. The lid keeps the splatter inside the bucket; toss the bag when finished. Rub the tool dry with a small towel.

4

Don't clean the brush with dish soap; it will gum up the ferrule and bristles. And there's no need to rinse the tool in fresh water. The more often you clean it with the softener solution, the better it gets. Fabric softener coats the handle, ferrule, and bristles, allowing paint to flow effortlessly off the tool. Magical!

Follow the same steps for rollers and paint pads. Rollers take a little more time, about 30 seconds, and they might require multiple dippings.

REMOVING OIL-BASED PAINTS

This cleaning method effectively strips oil-based materials from paintbrush bristles. Follow the steps carefully to avoid damaging the brush. You'll need about 20 seconds to clean oil-based paints from a brush, about 30 seconds from a roller.

If you wash out your expensive china bristle brushes in mineral spirits, they will become stiff due to paint residues left inside the bristles. This multi-step washout technique breaks down the oil-based paint and conditions the brush.

1. Start with three clean glass jars (such as mayonnaise jars) with lids that have a seal. Fill jar No. 1 about two-thirds full of mineral spirits. Fill jar No. 2 with a 50-50 solution of mineral spirits and denatured alcohol. Fill jar No. 3 with pure denatured alcohol. Mark each jar. If you are cleaning paint rollers, paint pads, or other tools that won't fit into the jars, use lidded buckets.

2. Scrape off excess paint using the edge of a 5-in-1 tool.

3. Dip the brush into jar No. 1 and swish it around for about 10 seconds. This is the "hottest" solution and will remove about 70 percent of the paint from the tool. Use a brush and roller spinner to spin the excess out of the brush into an empty bucket.

4. Dip the brush into jar No. 2, swish it around for about 10 seconds, then remove and spin. The mineral spirits dissolve the binders; the alcohol begins to strip out the oils. This will remove about 20 percent more.

5. Dip the brush in jar No. 3, swish for 10 seconds, remove, and spin. At this point, the natural oils have been stripped from the bristles, leaving them brittle and open, so they must be reconditioned.

6. Finish by swishing the brush for about 10 seconds in the liquid fabric softener mixture made following the recipe on page 129. This neutralizes the alcohol and conditions the bristles by restoring their oils. Rub the tool dry with a small towel.

Tips 'N' TRICKS

We all have one—a mucked-up water-based tool that wasn't cleaned properly before it was put away. Here's how to resurrect that old brush so it looks and works as good as new. Mix equal parts water, ammonia, and liquid fabric softener in a glass baking pan. Lay the brush in the mixture for 24 to 36 hours. Take it out and scrub off any stubborn paints. Finish by using the water-based washout method. Repeat until the brush is clean and then store it properly. For a quick solution, use spray oven cleaner; the lye will dissolve the old paint. The most extreme way to clean a tool is to use lacquer thinner, but use this powerful solvent carefully and sparingly.

CLEANING ROLLER COVERS

When you are finished painting, clean the excess paint from the roller cover using the curved edge of a 5-in-1 tool. Follow the directions for cleaning water-based or oil-based paint given on the preceding pages.

DISPOSABLE PAINT ROLLERS

I admit it: Disposable roller covers are more convenient for some jobs. To pull it off the frame, put the roller inside a plastic bag, grab the cover through the bag, pull it off, then seal the bag for disposal. Clean the roller frame appropriately for the type of paint you used. Oil the frame with a little spray lubricant and hang it up.

STORAGE Solutions

Proper storage preserves the investment you've made in paint and tools, and it makes it easier to find everything you need when it's time to begin a new paint project.

STORING PAINT

To store your paint so it lasts a lifetime, follow these steps:

1. If a paint can is less than one-half full, transfer excess paint to a smaller container. The storage rule is no more than one-third air space to two-thirds liquid. You can purchase gallon- and quart-size metal paint cans from a home supply store. Pour the paint through a nylon stocking to strain it. Label where you bought the paint, its type, color, sheen, mix number, and the storage date.

2. Using a plastic bag or the leftover curved part of your homemade Wizard apron (page 34), cut a circle 1 inch larger than the diameter of the paint can. This plastic circle will serve as a gasket to prevent moisture in the paint from corroding the lid of the can. It also plugs the holes that you punched in the can rim earlier. Most importantly, when you open the can to reuse the paint, you can easily scrape the pigments that have settled on the plastic back into the can.

3. Apply nonstick vegetable spray to one side of the plastic. It lubricates the rim, seals the lid, and prevents a skin from forming on the paint.

4. This step sounds odd, but it is essential in storing paint: Breathe into the can three times. The carbon dioxide from your breath forces out oxygen that is left in the can. Remember Law of Painting No. 3: The enemy of paint is air (or oxygen, to be more specific).

5. Place the plastic gasket over the top of the paint can, sprayed side down. Gently tap the lid closed using a rubber mallet, which is less likely to deform the lid or rim. Tap the lid flush with the rim. Place a rag over the can before striking to prevent splatters.

6. Store the paint can upside down to keep air from seeping into the can and to prevent a skin from forming. Store paint about 18 inches off the floor in a room, such as a basement, where the temperature averages about 50 degrees year-round. Keep paint locked away from children and never store it near a source of ignition, such as a pilot light or open flame. Both latex and oil-based paints can explode—I've seen it happen.

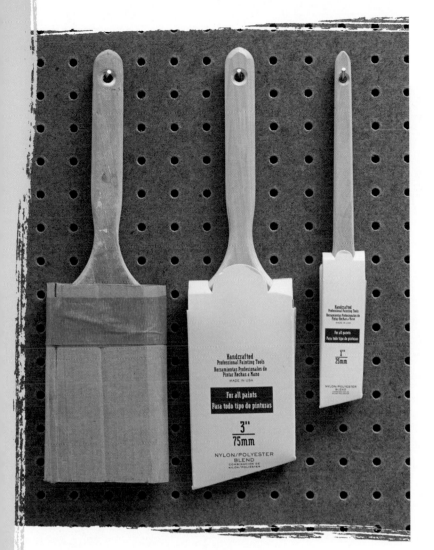

STORING PAINTBRUSHES

It's not enough just to clean brushes; you should also store them properly to keep the bristles from being damaged. The best and easiest way I know is to slip the dry brush back into its original plastic or cardboard cover. If you threw away the cover, you can make another one from light cardboard. Measure around the ferrule of the brush and add about 3 inches. Cut a piece of cardboard that wide and slightly longer than the distance from the top of the ferrule to the end of the bristles. Wrap the cardboard loosely around the brush and tape it. Slide the brush inside.

If you are as organized as I am, you can even color-code the brush covers. I use red for oil-based china bristle brushes and blue for water-based latex brushes. Finally, hang your paintbrush to store it—that's what the hole in the handle is for!

Wizard WARNING

Have you heard about wrapping paintbrushes in foil and storing them in the freezer? That's a horrible idea! Water-based paint is ruined in freezing conditions; nylon bristles become brittle and break; and a wet wooden handle will crack. If you want to store brushes temporarily during a paint project, wrap them in plastic so the paint and bristles are completely covered. Properly clean brushes for long-term storage.

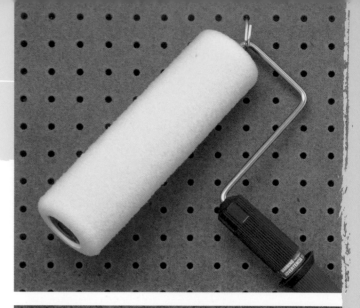

STORING ROLLERS AND PADS

Paint rollers

After roller covers have been spun and dried, the best way to store them is to put them back on the roller frame and hang the roller handle from a nail. That way, the roller is suspended in midair and will dry evenly and hold its shape.

Paint pads

Some pads are good only for two or three applications, others may last longer—it all depends on the quality of the pad and the nature of the surface on which it was used. Inspect the pads before storing and discard any that show wear (retain the handle and buy a new pad for your next job). To keep the pads fluffy, store them bristle side up. Never store solvent-soaked materials indoors. They release harmful fumes and can catch fire easily.

Quiz the Wiz

Can I save the paint I poured out of the can?

Absolutely, but don't just pour it back into the can from your bucket. Stretch a piece of nylon stocking over the opening of the can to strain any contaminates that dropped into the paint or were carried to it by your brush. Throw away the stocking when finished.

How can you tell if paint is no longer good?

Many factors can damage paint. Air contamination causes paint to dry and rust particles to form in the can. Unsatisfactory environmental conditions break the binders that help the paint adhere to a surface. Heat actually "cooks" the paint. Water-based paint that's been frozen undergoes a chemical change that can impede its bonding ability, breaking down the color pigments. Typically it is difficult to salvage paint that has gone bad.

Before applying any paint that's been stored for more than a month, smell it. A mildew or earthy smell indicates there's mold growing in the paint, which will inhibit proper application. Then check the paint's consistency. If it is more viscous than new paint, part of its ingredients have evaporated and the paint is no longer usable. If it appears unusually thin or runny, it means that the paint has separated. Old paint has a tendency to separate into its component parts; once it does so, it is difficult to obtain the same bonding properties. Dispose of it properly.

The Dish on **DISPOSAL**

Paint products are not as hazardous as they once were, but they still require special disposal. This often means taking them to an authorized household hazardous waste disposal site. Never pour them down the drain, into a storm sewer, onto the ground, or throw them into the trash. The secret is to convert paint products from a liquid state to a dry condition.

Water-based products

Water-based paints and strippers can be disposed of safely in the trash once their solvents evaporate. To dispose of them this way, apply the paint on a large sheet of plastic spread out and secured on a level surface. Heavy-duty .6-mil black plastic is a good choice because it is nonporous and dries the paint faster. Work with no more than one quart of paint at a time. Let the first coat dry and then spread out more paint. When all the paint has been spread and dried, fold the plastic sheet up and toss it into the trash. Leave the lids off empty latex paint cans until the paint residue inside dries and then toss the buckets into the trash.

Washout waste water

Let washout water sit overnight in the bucket. Once the dissolved paint materials have settled, gently pour off the water down the sink or toilet. Spread the remaining sludge from the bottom of the bucket on a large sheet of .6-mil. black plastic to dry out. Rinse and wipe out the inside of the bucket with lacquer thinner and allow it to dry.

Tips 'N' **TRICKS**

Instead of disposing of leftover paint at the dump, donate it to your local high school or college drama department, community center, or neighborhood housing organization.

Oil-based solvents

Oil-based solvents can be stored and used for years if sealed and stored properly. Solvents such as paint thinners can be refreshed and reused repeatedly. and that's good for the environment and for your wallet.

When solvents rest undisturbed for several days they will separate by their chemical makeup, specific density, and material composition. Because the materials in paint will settle to the bottom, the solvents will clarify on top. When the paint materials fill the containers about half way, pour off the clear solvent for reuse. Leave the lids off the jars and allow the solid material to harden and dry thoroughly, then dispose of them properly as solid waste. Contact your local solid waste disposal office for further information about safely disposing of or recycling leftover paint, used paint buckets, petroleum-based solvents, and other materials.

For safety, mobility, and long-term storage, place the glass jars in a large plastic storage bin with lid. Mark the bin with red duct tape and write "CAUTION—Oil-based Washout Storage Container—CAUTION" across the tape so there is no mistaking what it is. Tightly pack crumpled newspapers around the glass jars to absorb spills and to prevent glass breakage. After using the container, tightly close the jars, allow the newspaper dry out from any spills, and close up the storage container. Store it in a cool, dry, and secure place.

Wizard WARNING

Dispose of oil or solvent-soaked rags safely and permanently. Fill a clean, 1-gallon metal paint can two-thirds full with a 50-50 mixture of water and liquid fabric softener. Stuff the rags in the bucket, seal it with a metal lid, and take the filled bucket to a hazardous waste disposal center. The water deprives the rags of the oxygen needed to spontaneously combust, and the fabric softener breaks the bonds of the oils and solvents, making them less volatile.

Proper storage of tools and materials protects your investment in them and sets the stage for an easy start and successful finish to your next painting project.

chapter 5

Magical Paint Effects

Does this story sound familiar? You saw decorative painting effects, such as sponging, ragging, woodgraining, or marbling, demonstrated on TV or read about them in magazines. Maybe you even attended a workshop at your local home improvement store. So you invested in some expensive tools and set aside precious time in your quest to create amazing faux finishes on the walls of your home.

But right away, you had problems. The colors you thought would work together seemed to change. The paint you were using dried too quickly. The fancy brushes and sponges you bought gooped and globbed. Your anxiety and frustration started to build. Finally, five hours later, you stepped back with great expectation to admire your hard work, and—you hated it!

The truth is, decorative painting effects are not easy. They require the four "Ps" for success—Planning, Procedure, Patience, and Practice. Mostly practice, practice, and more PRACTICE!

This chapter showcases basic application techniques that will help you understand the concepts, controls, and character needed for decorative effects. Successful decorative painting, however, is the result of knowing and using the fundamentals of preparation and following the Three Laws of Painting—concepts that are covered in detail in the first four chapters of this book. So if you've skipped ahead to this chapter, make sure you go back and equip yourself with basic painting knowledge. Only then will you be mentally, physically, and technically ready to tackle decorative effects. I've spent 25 years making the same mistakes you have made, and more, so I've learned a few Wall Wizard tricks along the way—tricks that I'm going to share with you, so you too can create your own magical effects.

FAUX GET IT?
Decorative finishes add interest to any surface—page **140**

POSITIVE OR NEGATIVE
Two basic techniques create hundreds of finishes—page **146**

FAST, EASY EFFECTS
A sampler of faux effects to get you started—page **152**

FAUX *Get It?*

Faux effects are two-dimensional representations of the three-dimensional world. These painted illusions have height and width; the visual depth is created by using optical tricks such as scale and perspective, highlight and shadow. A scenic wall mural, a woodgrained door, or a painted inlaid table top are all examples of trompe l'oeil effects, a French term that means to fool the eye. If it's not the real deal, it's faux, or in other words a false finish.

A faux effect is an applied paint technique that simulates materials or imitates natural finishes. With the proper surface preparation, a faux effect can be applied on almost anything. The effects are created by painting a base coat of color, then layering different colors of semi-transparent glazes on top of the base coat.

Tips 'N' TRICKS

Faux effects are all about creating visual dimension where there is no physical dimension. Part of that effect is achieved by the nature of glaze itself—unlike paint, glaze is semi-transparent, allowing you to see through the top layer of the finish and glimpse the base coat underneath. But how much depth you perceive—something faux painters call the "depth of field" of a finish—depends on the degree of contrast between light and dark. In general, the higher the contrast between base coat and glaze, the greater the perceived depth of field.

*W*ith just 20 tools I can create more than 2,000 decorative effects, and they all boil down to this fact: Faux finishing is really about the colors you select and the way you use the tools. Here are some examples of basic finishes achieved with simple techniques using simple tools (there's more effects later in the chapter):

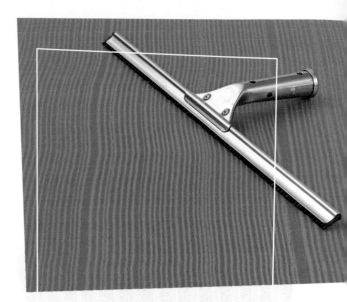

RAGGING TECHNIQUE

Ragging and rag-rolling are simply the application or removal (shown here) of a glaze over a base coat. The glaze shows the texture of the cloth rags or whatever other material you choose— burlap or plastic, for example.

COMBING TECHNIQUE

Combing is done by raking through a wet coat of colored glaze with various tools, allowing the base coat to show through in a pattern. You can cut a custom pattern into a standard window-washing squeegee (shown here). Paint and craft stores sell special combing tools.

SPONGING TECHNIQUE

Sponging colored glaze over paint is often done to create a random, mottled effect. The combinations of a base coat and a sponging color are unlimited, and you also sponge several colors onto one surface. Sponging can be used to remove glaze as well.

A simple way to understand how painting relates to faux effects is to imagine a tree. Basic painting represents the roots and the trunk of a tree. Faux effects represent two branches of that tree: positive techniques and negative techniques, both of which we'll discuss at length later. The specialty finishes are the tree's leaves: They're the decorative finishes that everyone sees, but in reality the trunk still holds the tree together. Underneath it all, the root system, or preparation, is what goes unseen but keeps the tree stable. You need to know the basics before you move on to the specialty effects.

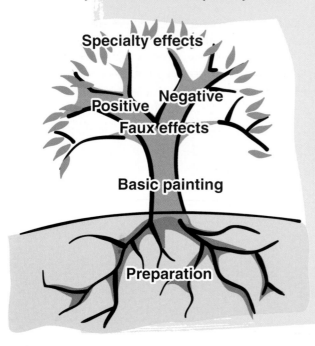

Specialty effects

Negative

Positive

Faux effects

Basic painting

Preparation

THE THREE C'S

What do I mean when I talk about the concept of faux effects? I'm referring to the color, style, furniture, and general design elements of a room that will guide you in choosing a faux effect. You must have a clear plan, or **concept,** to be successful in faux finishing.

Control is a question of mastering the medium. The control is the knowledge you have to produce an effect, as well as the tools that are used in this process. Hair clips, dish soap bottles, and sponge rollers are all examples of devices that help you control, or master, the medium of paint. Another aspect is how you control the ultimate painting tool—yourself. Be patient with yourself and your partner, and understand that you will make mistakes throughout the project. Your failure will ultimately bring success. This doesn't mean you can't experiment. In fact, some of my best finishes have been the result of mistakes. Make sure that you feel comfortable and confident with the technique and tool before tackling an entire room. Remember, when you believe, you can achieve the magic.

The result of how much control you have is what **character** is all about. The character of the effect is the end result of your project. It's a combination of planning, procedures, and the choices you make in your project partner, faux finish tool, and your willingness to practice and make mistakes. You must be happy with your results; if not, keep practicing until you are satisfied with the character of your project.

Tips 'N' **TRICKS**

No FEAR—*No Frustration, No Effort, No Anxiety, and No Resistance* to a project. Surprisingly, your greatest successes arise when you turn yourself over to the realm of possibilities. With No FEAR, a Wizard can move to the next step of taking RISKS. That means *Taking Responsibility, Taking Interest, Taking Self-Control, Taking Knowledge to understand the project, and Taking Satisfaction away from the project.* When you take RISKS, you'll reap the rewards. The more you do, the better you get.

The *RIGHT TOOLS*

In addition to common painting tools such as paintbrushes, rollers, and plastic paint pans, decorative finishes require specialty tools to create certain effects. But that doesn't mean you have to go out and spend a hundred bucks for a leather-look kit. In fact, some of the wackiest household tools create the most luxurious faux finishes. Remember to think off the wall and out of the can.

The Right Tool Rule means that things with handles, things made of plastic, and things that leave an impression are the most suitable for creating simple faux effects. A tool with a handle gives you a mechanical advantage, and it distances you from the surface you are working on. Why does this matter? You can see the effect emerge more clearly, and you keep yourself from being covered with glaze. Plastic is the easiest material to clean. Things that leave an impression offer an array of finishes that play upon highlight and shadow and create the optical illusion of depth in your faux effect.

It is also important to consider scale and perspective when choosing a tool to make an impression. The larger the tool, the larger the imprint. If used in a small room, a large tool can create a dramatic and sometimes overwhelming effect. When used in a larger room, the impression is proportional to the space.

BIGGER TOOL, BOLDER EFFECT

In conventional painting, tool size relates purely to applying paint in the most accurate, efficient manner. Faux painting, however, uses varying size tools for varying effect. Here a broom-and-squeegee tool sold to spread and level driveway sealer is used to create a striated pattern. Cut notches in the rubber squeegee side and draw it down the wall to create a big, bold stripe pattern—in no time!

What Lies **BENEATH**

Regardless of the effect you want to create, the first step in faux finishing is to paint a base coat on the wall. If you are a novice, begin with only two colors, then incorporate more complex combinations as you master a technique. Follow three rules when choosing a base coat:

☆ Always paint the darker color on the wall. OK, maybe not always, but if you're a novice, it is so much easier if the dark color is on the wall because it is easier to lighten a color than darken it. Use the lighter color in the top coat of glaze. This creates the illusion of a three-dimensional surface with highlights on top and shadows underneath.

☆ Use satin or eggshell interior latex paint for your base coat (see page 91). Flat paint sucks—literally—because of its high porosity; it has no sheen value. On the other hand, satin latex paint has a slight sheen that is ideal for decorative effects.

☆ Allow the base coat to dry completely before applying the top coat of glaze, a minimum of 4 to 8 hours. If you don't, the chemicals in the top coat of glaze can dissolve the base coat of paint. I usually paint the base coat the day before I create the faux finish.

Sealer

Base coat

Glaze and effect

Quiz the Wiz

How far in advance can I paint the base coat?
You can wait no more than a week before painting your faux finish on top of your base coat. Waiting longer will jeopardize the paint job because of everyday contaminants, such as hair spray, cooking oil, and general dust buildup. These contaminants put a film on the clean surface and prevent proper adhesion of the glaze.

What if I already have a satin finish on the wall?
You can apply glaze over an existing satin finish, but you need to clean it with a TSP solution first (page 67).

That Glazed **LOOK**

Glazes modify the color of a base coat of paint by allowing it to peek through a translucent filter. Think of glaze as the lens in sunglasses. You can see through tinted lens, but the view is altered. Use a glaze when you want to create visual depth of highlight and shadow.

Here's the main reason people buy this book—for the recipe of my amazing Wall Wizard Glaze. If you mix as directed, you'll have the perfect potion for faux finishing.

☆ One-half quart satin or eggshell latex interior paint. Remember to use the lighter color of your two-color combination.

☆ Two quarts glazing medium. This glazing medium is actually paint without color. It pulls the paint color molecules apart to create the translucent or semi-translucent effect of glaze.

☆ One-half quart water. Water is the thinning medium that makes it easier to work with the glaze.

☆ 6 ounces Floetrol. A binding medium, Floetrol is a Wall Wizard wonder. It stops blistering, cracking, mold, and mildew. It makes the color last three to four years longer, and it conditions the paint, making it sticky and gooey so the glaze sticks to the wall without running. Floetrol can be found at any home supply store.

☆ 4 drops fabric softener or ¼ teaspoon per gallon of paint. This household product acts as an extending agent, preventing the glaze from drying too quickly.

Combine all ingredients in a clean, 1-gallon juice jug and shake for about three minutes before using to keep the mixture from separating. In fact, every time you pick up the jug or dishsoap bottle, give it a shake before using—just make sure the lid is sealed tightly.

A 1-gallon juice jug makes the perfect container because it is made of plastic, so it won't corrode. It has a handle and an airtight seal, both of which are ideal for storing paint. And it holds enough glaze for 1,500 square feet, which will cover approximately two 10×15-foot rooms.

To make more or less glaze, use 1 part paint color to 4 parts glazing medium. The remaining ingredients are proportionate to this recipe.

How much glaze do you need? Enough to cover your project! Seriously, you will never ever be able to match a paint color, so if you run out of glaze before you finish, you might as well start over. Always make twice as much glaze as you think you will need.

Tips 'N' **TRICKS**

Instead of lugging around a gallon of glaze, fill a 1-quart dish soap bottle. The bottle has an airtight seal, it's easy to control, you can squeeze out just the amount you need, and most importantly, if you drop it, you won't get glaze all over everything!

BURNT SIENNA 124

POSITIVE or NEGATIVE

Faux finishes can be divided into either positive or negative techniques. Loading a tool with glaze and applying it to the wall is a positive technique—you are adding glaze to the wall. Covering the wall with a coat of glaze and then using a tool to remove it is a negative technique because you are taking glaze away. No matter which faux finish you want to achieve, you will use either a positive or negative technique to do so.

☆ Start on a practice wall to master your technique. Laundry rooms and guest rooms are a good choice—not the living room or kitchen where your mistakes will be visible. Be sure to prep the wall.

☆ Always dampen your tool in a solution of fabric softener and water (page 129) to prevent the glaze from sticking to the tool. The solution also softens the tool to make it the paint application easier. To make sure the tool is not too wet, cover the tool with a towel and wring out the excess solution.

☆ Make sure the molding is covered with tape or plastic so you can get into corners with your faux finish tool.

☆ Have two tools on hand: one to use and one that is drying while you work. When one tool is saturated with paint, clean it in a solution of fabric softener and water, then use the other tool while the first one dries.

PREP PROWESS

An ounce of prevention is worth ten pounds of cure. Basic painting techniques definitely apply when faux finishing. Mask moldings and windows with blue tape and masking film, and be sure to cover the floor with drop cloths, because the paints and glazes can drip and splatter easily.

When faux finishing, you will come in contact with the paint medium much more than when doing basic painting. It is also a good idea to be dressed to paint (page 34). Make sure the room is well-lit with industrial work lights so you can see what you are doing. Ventilation is essential, and the more open space you have to work, the less you'll have to stop and get out of your rhythm during painting.

Finally, never begin faux finishing in the middle of your living room. Make sure to practice, practice, practice the technique. Work vertically and fill a piece of 4×8-foot drywall or work in a room that is outside heavy traffic areas. Remember the Three C's: concept, control, and character.

Tips 'N' TRICKS

Here's the faux finish formula of success: Fifty percent of the effect—the way the faux finish will look—is derived from the base coat or foundation. Thirty percent of the finished effect is derived from the glazing medium and its interplay with the base coat. Ten percent of the effect is created by the application tool and the impression it makes. Ten percent is created by you and your application style.

DECORATIVE FINISHES

Technique	Tool	Comments
Texturing	Sea wool sponge Car mop	This technique creates texture on a wall. The texture depends on the tool you use.
Placement	Cling wrap Terry-cloth rags	This technique creates a stippled effect on the wall.
Appliqué	Foam stamps Stencils	Appliqué is adding a specific design to a wall to create a detail, or character point, in the room.

FAUX EFFECTS

Technique	Tool	Comments
Combing	Plastic hair comb Window squeegee	A dragging technique. Grooves or notches cut into rubber edge create the effect; the bigger the grooves, the wider the stripes.
Stippling	Feather duster Barbecue brush	When you dance the duster over the wall, the tool lifts the glaze from the wall, leaving the base coat to peek through. This method creates dimension.
Rolling	Roller with terry-cloth rag Bubble wrap	Attach rag or wrap to roller with rubber bands. Work in random pattern, rolling from a variety of directions to pick up the glaze.

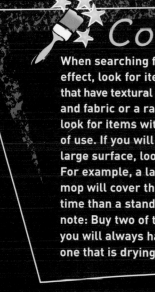

Cool TOOL

When searching for a tool to create an effect, look for items made of plastic that have textural elements like bristles and fabric or a raised surface. Also look for items with a handle for ease of use. If you will be working on a large surface, look for large items. For example, a large, industrial dust mop will cover the surface in less time than a standard dust mop. A note: Buy two of the same tool so that you will always have one to use and one that is drying while you work.

Here are some other tools to consider:

Toilet brush	Sea wool sponge
Tongs	Squeegee
Fly swatter	Bubble wrap
Truck tire brush	Terry-cloth
Duster car mop	Barbecue brush

As I mentioned earlier, sometimes the wackiest items make the best effects. Where do I look for tools? In the automotive and household cleaning sections—you'll never look at K-Mart or Wal-Mart in the same way again!

POSITIVE Thinking

Positive techniques in decorative finishing are the hardest to achieve because you have to get the effect even. It requires tactile response, the feedback you receive from the pressure you put on the tool. More pressure on the tool creates less detail because the tool, a sponge for example, is compressed against the wall. Less pressure creates more detail, because the points of the sponge surface make contact.

It usually takes three tries to get the hang of a technique: Your first try will be a failure; your second will be better; by the third you'll start to see the effect you want.

1. Lay out two plastic plates and squeeze glaze onto one. Use masking tape to attach the other to your "off" hand.

2. Load the tool by dipping it into the glaze three times: "Dippy, dippy, dippy."

3. Unload or lighten the load of glaze on the tool by tapping it on a clean plate three times: "Tappy, tappy, tappy." This also serves to distribute the glaze evenly on the tool.

Cool TOOL

A transport tray makes it easier to move around the room and paint. To make your own, cover a TV tray with about 15 sheets of aluminum foil. Squeeze the paint or glaze onto the aluminum foil and load your tool from that puddle. When the paint starts to dry and get sticky, or if you need to blend another color, all you have to do is peel away the top layer for a clean surface.

4

5

4. Gently touch the wall with the tool, keeping your hand parallel to the wall as you work. The tool should move perpendicular to the surface.

5. Rotate your wrist one-quarter turn as if you were turning a door knob. Your process repeats over and over: Tap, pick up the tool, rotate, tap, pick up the tool, rotate, and so on, turning your hand to a different position each time. Reload the tool.

Work in a spiral motion in 4-foot sections instead of straight across to avoid making a pattern. Work from the bottom up and into your field of view. A positive finish looks best when it is randomly applied on the surface. Avoid creating rows, columns, or any sort of structure in the finish.

Painting from the PANTRY

Clamp a hair clip to a sponge to create the perfect handle. Clips are made of plastic, they make the sponge ergonomic so that it's easier to hold, and they make it simple to control the sponge during application. Clips make it a cinch to sponge in corners and hard-to-reach areas.

NEGATIVE *Finishes*

Negative techniques require two roles to create a successful faux finish: the glazer and the whacker. The glazer applies glaze to the wall from the floor up. The whacker "whacks" the wall from floor to ceiling with the tool to create the effect by removing glaze. You can do negative finishes solo, but the technique really works much better when you team up with another person.

Working as a pair makes the job go more quickly; you get better results when working in assembly-line fashion. The glazer cuts-in and rolls on the glaze; the whacker works four to six feet behind the glazer. Don't let one get too far ahead or behind; the glaze will dry and you will get out of rhythm.

Changing whackers in the middle of a project will completely change "the hand" (the effect), because different people apply different pressure and rotate their wrists differently while whacking a wall. If you must work alone, work in 4-foot-wide sections, floor to ceiling, so the glaze doesn't dry while you are applying the faux effect.

One of the great things about negative finishes is that if you make a mistake—while the glaze is still wet—you can simply "erase" it by reglazing over the area and whacking it again.

Above all, make sure you practice, practice, practice your techniques. The moment of truth comes when you apply the glaze to the wall for the first time. If you're already accustomed to working with the glaze, your results will be dramatically better.

RHYTHM AND TIME

Rhythm is an important part of faux finishing. Getting in the groove—that is, pacing and timing your application as you paint will help you control and create consistency throughout your effect. It's all about keeping the glaze wet from one section to the next as you work vertically and horizontally across the wall with your tool. A tip: Play music while you work. It makes it easier to establish rhythm in your technique.

Also make sure that you work in the direction in which you feel most comfortable. If two people are working on a project, then you both need to work in the same direction; it will be easier to keep your rhythm, balance, and coordination. And try to work directly in front of yourself—your field of vision and your control of the tool will be much better.

RAG ROLLING

1. Using an application tool (such as a brush or pad), cut in the first section of the wall to be glazed. This section is generally 4 to 6 feet wide, working from floor to ceiling.

2. Pour ½ inch of glaze into the well of a paint pan. Load a sponge roller evenly with glaze.

3. Working from the bottom up, apply glaze to the wall over the base coat. Use more pressure on the lead side of the roller to avoid snail trails in the paint. (See page 104 to learn more about basic painting.) The goal is to create an even, consistent coat of glaze on the wall.

4. To create the faux effect, begin removing glaze with the tool, working from the baseboard up in 4-foot-wide sections, 4 to 6 feet behind the glazer. Roll randomly at all different angles, picking up the tool between each stroke. Work continuously around the room in sections. If you must stop working, stop in a corner where the change won't be as apparent. If you are right-handed, you'll probably find it easier to work from left to right. The opposite is true for left-handers.

Quiz the Wiz

Can the base glaze dry before adding the second layer of glaze?

Yes. Dry stacking creates crisper patterning with stronger details.

Can I apply a second layer of glaze onto a wet coat of base glaze?

Yes, but only in small amounts and contrasting colors. Wet blending creates softer effects.

Basic FAUX EFFECTS

SPONGE POSITIVE

Sponging is a popular but tricky technique, because you're adding a second layer of paint to an existing layer, and slight variations in how much paint you load onto the sponge and how hard you "whack" the surface you're finishing show up in the final effect. Practice this one on a spare sheet of wallboard—several times, if you need to—until you get a feel for how much paint to load, how long it takes before you need to reload, and what a good, consistent, rhythmic "pounce" of the sponge feels like. Because of the finesse required, this effect is best confined to small areas, such as tabletops, countertops, and furniture.

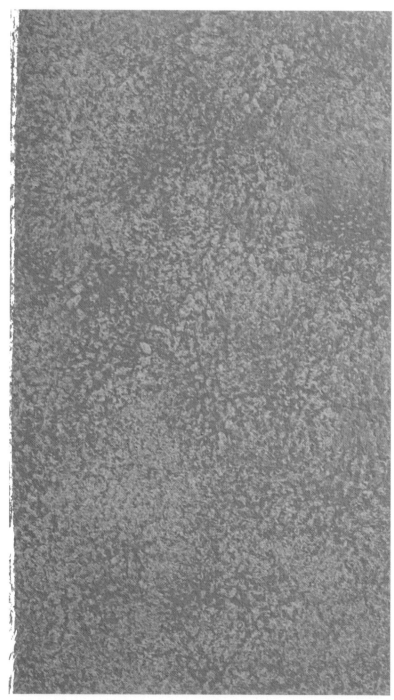

Finishes shown in this book are produced by four-color printing processes and may not match the colors of the paints actually used to create them. For an accurate color match, have the photograph scanned at a paint store or home improvement center.

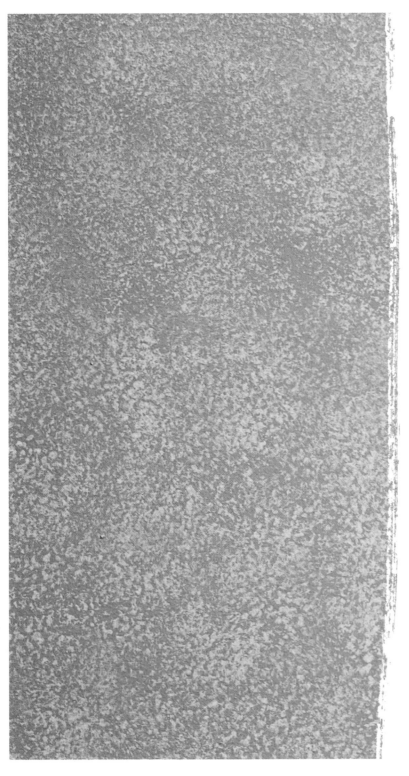

SPONGE NEGATIVE

Negative sponging is easier to learn and produces a much subtler, softer-looking effect than sponge positive. That's because you're lifting off glaze, rather than laying it down. You don't have to load the sponge, so you can work faster and create more consistent results. You can also mix different glazes for a rich, mottled effect.

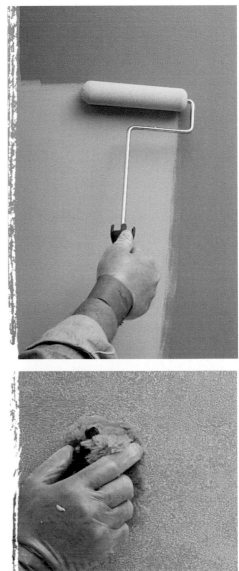

SPONGE NEGATIVE

The example of negative sponging on page 153 involved applying a lighter-colored glaze on a darker-colored background. The result had a dramatic, contrasty snap to it. The example on this page uses the same technique, but reverses the color layers. Here a darker glaze is applied over a lighter base coat. The result is a softer, more ethereal effect. The effect you choose is a matter of taste and desired result: What mood do you want to create in a room? Which elements do you want to stand out? If you want your walls to be noticed, apply dark glaze on a light base. If you want them to fade into the background, yet still have some depth and texture, choose a light glaze on a dark base.

MOP NEGATIVE

A mop is one of my favorite tools: It has a long handle, so it's easy to use, plus it's readily available, inexpensive, and easy to clean. Like a sponge, you can use it with both positive and negative techniques. Again, the negative is easier to learn and allows you to move faster than the positive technique. Mops come in various sizes, materials, and textures, so the variety of finishes you can produce with them is nearly endless. Since most mops have a coarser texture than sponges, the effects they produce will have a little more drama and depth to them than sponging. And they allow you to play with various scales of pattern. For a dramatic, notice-me effect, use a large mop on a small wall, with a high contrast between the base and the glaze coat. For a softer effect, use a small mop on a large wall, with only a one- or two-shade difference between the colors of the base and the glaze.

TIRE BRUSH NEGATIVE

I love this tool! Like a mop, a tire brush comes in a variety of sizes and bristle textures, each one allowing for a slightly different result. Pull the brush down across a wet glaze coat for striae (thin, parallel lines), as shown here. A striated pattern is the basis for faux wood-grain effects.

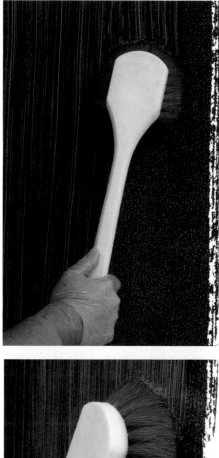

TIRE BRUSH SWIRL

Swirling a tire brush on a wet glaze—scouring or scrubbing the surface gently—is neither a positive nor negative technique, as glaze is neither added nor subtracted from the surface. Rather it is moved around randomly to create a subtle variation in the surface, giving a sense of depth or movement that's soothing, almost hypnotic—like gazing at a river's slowly swirling water.

STIPPLE BRUSH POSITIVE

Stippling—pouncing a brush repeatedly to apply or remove glaze from a surface—is the basis for faux stone effects. It simulates the random, speckled texture of rock, implying a three-dimensional, crystalline structure on a two-dimensional surface. Stippling is also the basis for sky and cloud effects, where light fades to dark, dark to light, or one color to another. Gradually increasing or decreasing the amount of glaze you add to the base as you move up or across the wall creates those effects, which convincingly imitate nature.

STIPPLE BRUSH NEGATIVE

Negative stippling isn't difficult but still requires practice to achieve an even, yet random, finish. Combine a light, even rhythm with random tool positioning. Hold the brush so the bristles are always perpendicular to the wall. Rotate the tool with each hit to avoid cornrows or patterns that distract from the dotted, grainy effect. You'll develop a feel for when to "pad off" the brush, tapping it on a dry towel a few times every so often to remove excess glaze from the bristles. You want to do that just before the effect starts to degrade, something you'll discover by trail and error.

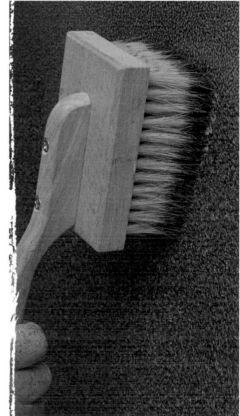

SQUEEGEE NEGATIVE

Using a squeegee to produce a negative combing effect is one of the simplest, most dramatic faux techniques you can use. Buy specially-made tools or make your own by notching a window squeegee. You can use it to create striae, as shown here, or swirl, herringbone, crosshatch, or basketweave effects, to name a few. The trick to using a squeegee is pressure consistency. You want firm enough pressure on the tool to draw through the glaze to the base coat, but not so much that you collapse the tool and take all the glaze off. Attach a handle to the squeegee for better control. The technique works best on smooth surfaces.

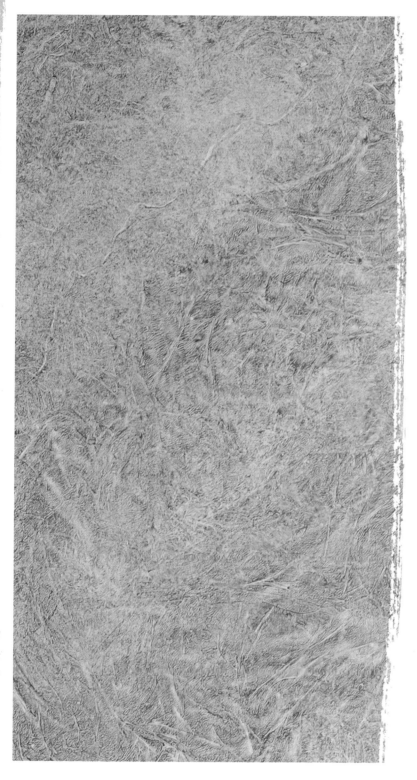

PLASTIC SHEET NEGATIVE

Plastic sheeting supplies the magic that lets you create a marble effect on walls, duplicating in just a few minutes a material that nature took millions of years to create. The trick is to use thin plastic: .5 mil is best. Have one person apply it to the glazed wall, another person crinkle and model it as it goes on. Work quickly and randomly—being too deliberate in your manipulations will result in a stiff, patterned appearance. For even more depth and variation, wad up the plastic after you pull it off and gently wipe it across the surface quickly and randomly to create subtle color drifts.

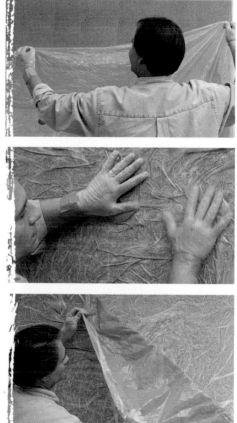

TIPS, TRICKS, TOOLS, and more ...

PREPARING TO PAINT

Paint a piece of white 24×30-inch foam-core board the desired color. When it's dry, use it to test the paint in a variety of light conditions and locations. Hold it vertically on the walls to view it. This method also lets you see how furniture and accessories in a room look when positioned against or next to a particular color. See page 22.

When patching white walls and molding, mix two drops of red food coloring into every 6 ounces of patching compound to make it easy to spot repairs for sanding later. See page 45.

Colored party toothpicks make it a snap to remount drapery hardware, towel bars, or picture hooks in a room. Pack toothpicks snugly into each hole you want to reuse. Then spackle the holes without picks. The toothpicks make the holes easy to find when it's time to reattach the hardware. See page 40.

Never begin a paint project in the public rooms in your home, such as the kitchen, dining room, living room, or any other rooms frequented by guests. Instead try out your colors and build your skill level in a laundry room, bathroom, or bedroom. Even a storage room or garage is a good place to experiment. See page 29.

Plastic wrap works magic. Use it to cover doorknobs and keep splatters off hardware. If you are painting the ceiling, press a sheet of plastic wrap over your eyeglasses. You can still see through them, but the wrap protects the lenses from paint drops. See page 35.

Here's a Wall Wizard solution for cleanup: baby wipes. See page 38.

As you disassemble the room, drop all the switch plates into one medium plastic bag. Remount screws back into their fixtures so they don't get lost or scratch the plastic plates. Separate the hardware for each window, door, and curtain into its own bag and mark its location in the room. Once all the hardware has been bagged and tagged, place the bags into one large bag with the room name on it. For safe keeping, stick the bag on the windowpane of the room with blue tape. See page 41.

Anything you don't want to get paint on, including yourself, should be covered. Make a trash bag apron from a 13-gallon tall kitchen plastic trash bag. See page 34.

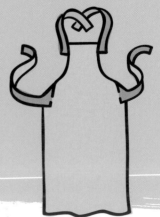

What can I do about that awful paneling in my living room?

My advice is to install ¼-inch drywall over the paneling to gain a clean, fresh surface (see page 54). If you do want to paint or paper over paneling, you must fill, sand, and prime; or cover the paneling with special liner paper. See page 53.

Thinking about painting over wallpaper? Think again! Wallpaper patterns and seam lines can show through the paint. Plus the paint can act as a solvent to the wallpaper paste, causing the paper to fall off the wall while you're painting or bubble, wrinkle, and release irregularly over time. See page 63.

Think your walls are grime-free? Try this test: Spray a tissue with water and lightly it rub on the wall. See that brown smudge? It's body oils, hair spray, and food oils that become airborne while cooking and eventually settle on the walls. Lots of paint jobs fail because new, clean paint is applied on top of dingy, dirty surfaces. Clean before you paint. See page 67.

Remove wallpaper with this Secret Stripping Solution

3 gallons hot water
22 ounces wallpaper remover concentrate
¼ cup liquid fabric softener
1 cup white vinegar
2 tablespoons baking soda
See page 65.

Heard the one about using toothpaste to fill holes in the wall? Here's the real story: Toothpaste doesn't hold up over time, and the color sparkles or bleaches can show through the paint over time. See page 43.

Instead of spending hours masking off window glass, rub lip balm around the inside of each pane. When the paint dries, take a knife and score around the glass, then scrape the paint and wax away. If you still have wax on the glass, heat the glass with a hair dryer and bluff clean. See page 72.

Any adhesive left on the wall can crackle the paint and prevent it from sticking successfully. To make sure you have removed all the adhesive, give the wall an iodine test. Mix 1 ounce of iodine with 1 quart of water. Use a trigger spray bottle to mist the wall. If the spray on the wall turns bluish purple, adhesive is still there and you need to continue cleaning. See page 66.

To keep paint from seeping under the edge of masking tape, heat-seal the tape. Run the end of a tapered plastic tool quickly over the applied edge of the blue masking tape after you've set the tape. This heats the edge of the tape, and the waxy adhesive on the tape melts. See page 73.

TIPS, TRICKS, TOOLS, and more ...

PAINTING LIKE A PRO

Have a cleanup bucket ready at the start of any painting project. Fill a 5-gallon bucket about two-thirds full of water and place a tile sponge in it. Place it in the middle of the room with a large towel beneath it. Use a damp sponge to absorb and clean up any spills. Change the water often. Have plenty of shop rags or towels around to soak up water spills. See page 76.

If you need to stop painting temporarily, protect the paint in your bucket or roller tray by slipping a plastic shower cap or plastic bowl cover over it. The cover keeps debris and air out. Put brushes in a resealable plastic bag. Tie closed the plastic trash bag you've used to line your paint bucket.

Line your paint pot with a large resealable plastic bag. Open the mouth of the bag and fold down over the edge of the bucket rim. Secure with a large rubber band. If you need to pause from painting, zip the bag closed to prevent drying. See page 100.

Paint the trim work first, then the walls. This strategy will make it easier to sand, prepare, and paint all the details, edges, and planes of the trim work. After all the coats of paint on the trim work are dry, mask off the trim work and paint the wall. See page 109.

Slide a metal roller tray into a heavy-duty tall plastic kitchen bag, then press the bag into the tray to create a liner. If you need to stop, fold the liner over the tray to keep the paint from drying. The bag liner makes cleanup a cinch; simply turn the bag inside out and toss it in the trash. See page 79.

Take the "pain" out of painting. To avoid carpal tunnel syndrome, blisters, and cramps, make a soft grip for your paintbrush. Take 2-inch diameter pipe insulation, trim to the right length, and shove it over the handle of your paintbrush. See page 77.

Build some bucket stilts See page 81.

Make a handy painting tool belt
See page 80.

For the best finish on trim, apply two thin coats of paint rather than one heavy coat. The first thin coat dries faster and bonds better to the surface. The second coat deepens the color coverage. With one heavy coat you run the risk of the paint sagging, creating a poor finish quality. See page 112.

To keep latex paint off your body, apply nonstick cooking spray onto your skin and rub it in. Water-based paint can't penetrate the oil, so the paint won't seep through your skin. I figure, if you can eat it, you can wear it: Just make sure you use the original flavor spray—not the garlic version!

Paint over textured surfaces with a foam roller. This type of roller will unload a lot of paint on an irregular surface. The foam conforms to the surface it is rolling on, working paint into to all the nooks and crannies, producing even surface coverage.

Don't like the smell of paint? To every quart of interior latex paint, add four drops of vanilla extract. You can also use other extracts, such as peppermint, as long as the alcohol in the ingredients is methyl alcohol, which is formulated to mix with water. Do not use perfume or other alcohol-based fragrances. See page 89.

Remove masking materials within 45 to 90 minutes after the paint is applied and set to prevent tearing the surface. When paint flows over the sealed edge of masking tape, then hardens, the paint film bonds to both the wall and the tape. It's easier to remask an area then to repair it! See page 110.

Make a paint tray trolley. Buy a large square plant dolly with casters, four 4- to 6-inch plastic spring clamps, and a length of 2-inch foam pipe insulation. Center an empty paint tray to the plant mover and pencil its outline of where the tray will be used. At the four points of the outline, secure a spring clamp to the plant dolly with screws. Make a wall bumper by applying the pipe insulation around the edge of the plant mover. To use, place a paint tray on the dolly and clamp in in place.

TIPS, TRICKS, TOOLS, and more ...

PAINTING LIKE A PRO

Instead of lugging around a gallon of glaze, fill a 1-quart dishsoap bottle. The bottle has an air-tight seal, it's easy to control, you can squeeze out just the amount you need, and most importantly, if you drop it, you won't get glaze all over everything! See page 145.

To paint wall switches and vent covers, wash them thoroughly and coat them with a white-pigmented sealer, such as Kilz, let dry, then paint with the finish color.

Even Wall Wizards have a hard time knowing what color is inside a nondescript can of paint. Dab the paint on the outside of the can. To make it easier to match the color when you touch up a room, dab a paint spot on the backside of a switch plate in the room and write the color name, number, and manufacturer on it.

Clamp a hair clip to a sponge to create the perfect handle. Clips are made of plastic, they make the sponge ergonomic so that it's easier to hold, and they make it simple to control the sponge during application. See page 149.

If you hate paint drips and splatters on your eyeglasses, cover them with plastic kitchen cling wrap. When splatters happen, simply remove the old and apply a new piece.

To create a crisp line between the wall and the ceiling when cutting in, apply a light strip of lip balm around the edge of the ceiling. The paint won't stick to the wax in the lip balm, and there is no need to remove it after the paint is dry.

A transport tray makes it easier to move around the room and paint. To make your own, cover a TV tray with about 15 sheets of aluminum foil. Squeeze the paint or glaze onto the aluminum foil and load your tool from that puddle. When the paint starts to dry and get sticky, or if you need to blend another color, all you have to do is peel away the top layer for a clean surface. See page 148.

CLEANUP, STORAGE, AND DISPOSAL

You can clean water-based paint from brushes and paint pads in 10 seconds. Here's how:

1. Remove excess paint from the brush or pad.
2. Add ½ cup of fabric softener per gallon of water. Mix several gallons.
3. Dip a brush into the mixture, swish briskly through the water, and count to 10.
4. Dry the brush using a paintbrush spinner. Spin the brush in a wet waste bucket. Rub the tool dry with a small towel.

See page 129.

To dispose of water-based paint, pour no more than 1 quart onto a large sheet of .6-mil black plastic. Let the first coat dry and then spread out more paint. When the paint has dried, fold the plastic sheet up and toss it into the trash. Leave the lids off empty latex paint cans until the paint residue inside dries and then toss the cans into the trash. See page 135.

Before applying any paint that has been stored for more than a month, smell it. A mildew or earthy smell indicates there's mold growing in the paint, which will inhibit proper application. Then check the paint's consistency. If it is more viscous than new paint, part of its ingredients have evaporated and the paint is no longer usable. If it appears unusually thin or runny, it means that the paint has separated. Old paint has a tendency to separate into its component parts; once it does so, it is difficult to obtain the same bonding properties. Dispose of it properly. See page 134.

Dispose of oil or solvent-soaked rags safely and permanently. Fill a clean, 1-gallon metal paint can two-thirds with a 50-50 mixture of water and liquid fabric softener. Stuff the rags in the bucket, seal it with a metal lid, and take the filled bucket to a hazardous waste disposal center. See page 136.

To store paint, place a piece of plastic garbage bag over the top of a paint can. Gently tap the lid closed over the plastic, using a rubber mallet. Store the paint can upside down to keep air from seeping into the can and to prevent a skin from forming. For more on paint storage, see page 132.

Have you heard about wrapping paintbrushes in foil and storing them in the freezer? That's a horrible idea! Water-based paint is ruined in freezing conditions; nylon bristles become brittle and break; and a wet wooden handle will crack. See page 133.

INDEX

INDEX CONTINUED

METRIC CONVERSIONS

U.S. UNITS TO METRIC EQUIVALENTS

To Convert From	Multiply By	To Get
Inches	25.4	Millimeters
Inches	2.54	Centimeters
Feet	30.48	Centimeters
Feet	0.3048	Meters
Yards	0.9144	Meters
Miles	1.6093	Kilometers
Square inches	6.4516	Square centimeters
Square feet	0.0929	Square meters
Square yards	0.8361	Square meters
Acres	0.4047	Hectares
Square miles	2.5899	Square kilometers
Cubic inches	16.387	Cubic centimeters
Cubic feet	0.0283	Cubic meters
Cubic feet	28.316	Liters
Cubic yards	0.7646	Cubic meters
Cubic yards	764.55	Liters
Fluid ounces	29.574	Milliliters
Quarts	0.9464	Liters
Gallons	3.7854	Liters
Drams	1.7718	Grams
Ounces	28.350	Grams
Pounds	0.4536	Kilograms

To convert from degrees Fahrenheit (F) to degrees Celsius (C), first subtract 32, then multiply by $\frac{5}{9}$.

METRIC UNITS TO U.S. EQUIVALENTS

To Convert From	Multiply By	To Get
Millimeters	0.0394	Inches
Centimeters	0.3937	Inches
Centimeters	0.0328	Feet
Meters	3.2808	Feet
Meters	1.0936	Yards
Kilometers	0.6214	Miles
Square centimeters	0.1550	Square inches
Square meters	10.764	Square feet
Square meters	1.1960	Square yards
Hectares	2.4711	Acres
Square kilometers	0.3861	Square miles
Cubic centimeters	0.0610	Cubic inches
Cubic meters	35.315	Cubic feet
Liters	0.0353	Cubic feet
Cubic meters	1.3079	Cubic yards
Liters	0.0013	Cubic yards
Milliliters	0.0338	Fluid ounces
Liters	1.0567	Quarts
Liters	0.2642	Gallons
Grams	0.5644	Drams
Grams	0.0353	Ounces
Kilograms	2.2046	Pounds

To convert from degrees Celsius to degrees Fahrenheit, multiply by $\frac{9}{5}$, then add 32.

CREDITS

Painting Secrets from Brian Santos, The Wall Wizard

Editor: Ken Sidey
Contributing Writers: Heidi Tyline King, Dan Weeks
Senior Associate Design Director: Doug Samuelson
Graphic Designer: Chad Owen
Copy Chief: Terri Fredrickson
Copy and Production Editor: Victoria Forlini
Editorial Operations Manager: Karen Schirm
Managers, Book Production: Pam Kvitne,
  Marjorie J. Schenkelberg, Rick von Holdt, Mark Weaver
Contributing Copy Editor: Stacey Schildroth
Contributing Proofreaders: Pamela Elizian, Juliet Jacobs,
  David Krause, Terri Krueger, Jina Nelson
Illustrator: Michael Burns
Photographers: Doug Hetherington, Bill Nellans
Indexer: Donald Glassman
Editorial and Design Assistants: Renee E. McAtee,
  Karen McFadden, Mary Lee Gavin

Meredith® Books

Editor in Chief: Linda Raglan Cunningham
Design Director: Matt Strelecki
Executive Editor, Gardening and Home Improvement:
  Benjamin W. Allen
Executive Editor, Home Improvement: Larry Erickson

Publisher: James D. Blume
Executive Director, Marketing: Jeffrey Myers
Executive Director, New Business Development: Todd M. Davis
Executive Director, Sales: Ken Zagor
Director, Operations: George A. Susral
Director, Production: Douglas M. Johnston
Business Director: Jim Leonard

Vice President and General Manager: Douglas J. Guendel

Meredith Publishing Group

President, Publishing Group: Stephen M. Lacy
Vice President-Publishing Director: Bob Mate

Meredith Corporation

Chairman and Chief Executive Officer: William T. Kerr

In Memoriam: E.T. Meredith III (1933-2003)

Copyright © 2004 by Meredith Corporation, Des Moines,
  Iowa. First Edition.
All rights reserved. Printed in the United States of
  America.
Library of Congress Control Number: 2003106478
ISBN: 0-696-21759-7

All of us at Meredith® Books are dedicated to providing
you with the information and ideas you need to enhance
your home and garden. We welcome your comments and
suggestions. Write to us at:
Meredith Books
Home Improvement Books Department
1716 Locust St.
Des Moines, IA 50309–3023

If you would like to purchase any of our home
improvement, gardening, cooking, crafts, or home
decorating and design books, check wherever quality
books are sold. Or visit us at: bhgbooks.com

Note to the Readers: Due to differing conditions, tools,
and individual skills, Meredith Corporation assumes no
responsibility for any damages, injuries suffered, or losses
incurred as a result of following the information published
in this book. Before beginning any project, review the
instructions carefully, and if any doubts or questions
remain, consult local experts or authorities. Because
codes and regulations vary greatly, you always should
check with authorities to ensure that your project
complies with all applicable local codes and regulations.
Always read and observe all of the safety precautions
provided by manufacturers of any tools, equipment, or
supplies, and follow all accepted safety procedures.

DEDICATION

To all people who need to know the why behind the how-to. Remember, your house is your castle, but it takes a little magic to make it a home.

Thank-yous

It takes a village to raise a Wizard. My special thanks ...

To my mom, for her artistic influence. To my dad, for his work ethics, and to my grandfather for instilling in me the power of "why."

To the Meredith Corporation, especially Ken, Ben, and Doug, for their belief in the "magic" of the Wizard.

To my children, Paul, Scott, and Kelli, whom I love, and who are the future.

And most of all, to my wife and partner, Virginia, who shares all my "dreams." Thank you for all your love and support throughout our journeys together.

NOTES

NOTES